Welcome

Everybody needs, and deserves, a break. But what if you want to do something more for mind, body and soul, than simply lie on a beach or take in the sights of a city? This guide to travelling mindfully features inspiring activities to help you reconnect with your inner peace, resort destinations that are set up with spas, yoga and wellness practices to relax and rejuvenate, and locations where you can get back to nature and embrace the restful and healing powers of forests, the countryside, the coast, and more. From the latest Californian wellness trends to the tried-and-true value of a walk in the British countryside, there's something here to help everyone relax, unwind, and make the most of every moment of rest.

DISCLAIMER

The Coronavirus pandemic has had a dramatic impact on global travel. As such, the locations, activities and websites mentioned within may no longer be available or appropriate. Always check the current travel guidelines when planning a trip, and adhere to any local restrictions. With ongoing conflicts and humanitarian crises, it's also important to check the latest foreign travel advice for your destination.

Readers rely on any information at their sole risk, and this book, and its publisher, Future Publishing Ltd, limit their liability to the fullest extent permitted by law.

FUTURE

MINDFUL TRAVEL

Future PLC Quay House, The Ambury, Bath, BA1 1UA

Editorial
Editor **April Madden**
Designer **Emma Wood**
Compiled by **Zara Gaspar & Briony Duguid**
Senior Art Editor **Andy Downes**
Head of Art & Design **Greg Whitaker**
Editorial Director **Jon White**

Cover images
Getty Images
Illustration by Katy Stokes

Photography
All copyrights and trademarks are recognised and respected

Advertising
Media packs are available on request
Commercial Director **Clare Dove**

International
Head of Print Licensing **Rachel Shaw**
licensing@futurenet.com
www.futurecontenthub.com

Circulation
Head of Newstrade **Tim Mathers**

Production
Head of Production **Mark Constance**
Production Project Manager **Matthew Eglinton**
Advertising Production Manager **Joanne Crosby**
Digital Editions Controller **Jason Hudson**
Production Managers **Keely Miller, Nola Cokely, Vivienne Calvert, Fran Twentyman**

Printed by William Gibbons, 26 Planetary Road, Willenhall, West Midlands, WV13 3XT

Distributed by Marketforce, 5 Churchill Place, Canary Wharf, London, E14 5HU
www.marketforce.co.uk Tel: 0203 787 9001

Mindful Travel Third Edition (LBZ5037)
© 2022 Future Publishing Limited

We are committed to only using magazine paper which is derived from responsibly managed, certified forestry and chlorine-free manufacture. The paper in this bookazine was sourced and produced from sustainable managed forests, conforming to strict environmental and socioeconomic standards. All contents © 2022 Future Publishing Limited or published under licence. All rights reserved. No part of this magazine may be used, stored, transmitted or reproduced in any way without the prior written permission of the publisher. Future Publishing Limited (company number 2008885) is registered in England and Wales. Registered office: Quay House, The Ambury, Bath BA1 1UA. All information contained in this publication is for information only and is, as far as we are aware, correct at the time of going to press. Future cannot accept any responsibility for errors or inaccuracies in such information. You are advised to contact manufacturers and retailers directly with regard to the price of products/services referred to in this publication. Apps and websites mentioned in this publication are not under our control. We are not responsible for their contents or any other changes or updates to them. This magazine is fully independent and not affiliated in any way with the companies mentioned herein.

Future plc is a public company quoted on the London Stock Exchange (symbol: FUTR)
www.futureplc.com

Chief executive **Zillah Byng-Thorne**
Non-executive chairman **Richard Huntingford**
Chief financial officer **Penny Ladkin-Brand**

Tel +44 (0)1225 442 244

Widely Recycled

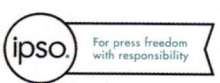
ipso. For press freedom with responsibility

Contents

DESTINATION INSPIRATION

- 10   *Wellness around the world*
- 14   *Six of the best... Mood-boosting breaks*
- 16   *10 feel good getaways*
- 22   *Eat well around the world*
- 24   *Hidden city gems*
- 28   *Six of the best... Parkruns in the world*
- 30   *Yes, you can afford a holiday home!*
- 34   *Far, far away*
- 40   *Six of the best... Waterside breaks*
- 42   *We're living the Mamma Mia dream!*
- 46   *Making memories that last a lifetime*

WONDERFUL WORLD

84	*Recharge in Palm Springs*
88	*Feel well in West Hollywood*
90	*A natural wonder*
92	*Magical Mexico*
96	*Paradise islands*
102	*Wild wellness in Mauritius*
104	*Breathtaking Cambodia*
108	*Off the beaten track*
110	*Million pound mountains*
112	*Living la dolce vita*
118	*Learn to live the bella figura*
120	*Recipe for success*
122	*Three go mad in Ibiza*
124	*Mountain mayhem!*

BEAUTIFUL BRITAIN

52	*Isles of wonder*
56	*Why there's no place better than the British countryside in summer*
58	*Literary landscapes*
64	*Six of the best... UK walking hotspots*
66	*Taking the waters*
70	*Six of the best... UK swim spots*
72	*It's a shore thing*
76	*Treasure island*

MINDFUL TRAVEL | 7

DESTINATION INSPIRATION

10   *Wellness around the world*
From sound healing to forest bathing, explore trends around the globe

14   *Six of the best... Mood-boosting breaks*
Booking one of these trips will put a well-earned smile on your face

16   *10 feel good getaways*
For a holiday that'll leave you rejuvenated and ready to face anything

22   *Eat well around the world*
Sampling the local produce could have more benefits than you think...

24   *Hidden city gems*
Discover these celebrated spots and fabulous finds in four destinations

28   *Six of the best... Parkruns in the world*
Free, weekly, timed 5km runs around the world. Here are our favourites...

30   *Yes, you can afford a holiday home!*
Achieving the two-home dream is more affordable than you think...

34   *Far, far away*
Feast your eyes on the stunning scenery of these dream destinations

40   *Six of the best... Waterside breaks*
There's always something incredibly soothing about staying by the water...

42   *We're living the Mamma Mia dream!*
Three W&H readers who've upped sticks and moved to an island paradise

46   *Making memories that last a lifetime*
A holiday is the perfect time to create meaningful moments

10

34

WELLNESS *around the* WORLD!

From sound healing to forest bathing, these wellness trends from all corners of the globe promise to relax, revitalise and reset your senses…

Whether it's aromatherapy, investing in your diet and fitness routine, or simply running a bath **as a way of carving out a little "me time", there's no denying the rising popularity of wellness.** According to the latest statistics from the Global Wellness Institute, the industry is worth approximately £3.3 trillion – and it's showing no sign of slowing. But why are we so drawn to the wellbeing wave?

A study from course directory obby.co.uk found that 45% of British workers do little or nothing at all to relieve work stress. Couple that with the rise of technology and a faster pace of life, and it's no wonder we want to retreat, hit pause and reassess our wellbeing. "It's worrying how many people claim they don't prioritise getting the stress relief that is so important for maintaining good mental health," says Tom Batting, co-founder of Obby. Yet we all know the benefits of taking some me time and escaping from the stresses and strains of today's busy lifestyles. Need to wind down? Here's how people do it from around the world.

WELLNESS AROUND THE WORLD

LIVE LONGER LIKE THE JAPANESE

According to the World Health Organization, Japanese women have the longest life expectancy, with an average lifespan of 86.8 years. So what is their secret? "It's a combination of factors, including diet, a sense of community and living in rhythm with the seasons," says Beth Kempton, author of Japanese wellbeing book *Wabi Sabi* (£12.99, Piatkus). "People in Japan have a deep aesthetic sense, which leads to them finding joy in small things," she explains. "To live inspired by Japanese culture and lifestyle means to pay attention to details in the world around us, to be considerate of each other, quiet at times, and embrace simplicity."

The Japanese practice of "forest bathing", or "shinrin-yoku", is making waves in the wellness world. It involves taking time out to walk and wonder in nature without distractions from today's modern technology.

"The benefits of getting out into fresh air and away from city pollutants are endless," says Kay Pennington, Aqua Sana group spa manager. "Not only is it wonderful for your mental wellbeing, but breathing in clean air from plants is a powerful way to avoid harmful toxins and ensure your body works at its very best."

SOUTH KOREA'S HEALING COFFEE

Need a pick-me-up? Most of us will down one of the 95 million cups of coffee that are drunk in the UK every day. But in Korea, they get more than a caffeine fix with their daily brew. Yes, their morning latte comes with a side of therapy too (and we don't mean in chocolate brownie form, either!). Say hello to healing cafés.

"An increased awareness of mental health is giving rise to public spaces designed to recharge and rebalance in hectic cities," says Lucie Greene, director of JWT Innovation, a trend forecasting business. South Korean employees work some of the longest hours in the world, so these relaxation coffee shops act as a public place for time-poor people to decompress and relax, with massage chairs, napping pods and ambient music to accompany your drink. "New spaces are opening up to promote mental wellbeing, replacing traditional cafés as popular public hangouts while capitalising on the buzzy self-care industry."

HEALTHY EATING FROM HAWAII

Intuition and the senses are core to Hawaiian culture. "The Polynesians, for instance, sailed and mapped the Pacific Ocean through use of their senses," explains Karuna Wiese, an intuitive therapist, speaker and founder of Hub for the Heart (hubfortheheart.com), who has lived in Hawaii for over 20 years.

One way the Hawaiians channel this intuition is through intuitive eating. This involves listening to their body and its needs, and then eating a diet that supports it. Hawaii is also known as the "healing island", with locals often using organic and locally sourced food and drink as natural remedies.

One beverage that is growing in popularity is jun, a fermented drink (known as the "champagne kombucha"), which is created on a base of green tea, honey and good bacteria cultures. "Jun is becoming popular in Hawaii due to its whole support of body, brain and spirit," explains Karuna. Health benefits include boosting the immune system and supporting healthy bacteria in the gut, which is key for healthy brain function. While the origins of jun are uncertain, it's rumoured to have been a favourite fermented health drink of Tibetan monks, who would meditate and pray while this mysterious elixir brewed.

MINDFUL TRAVEL | 11

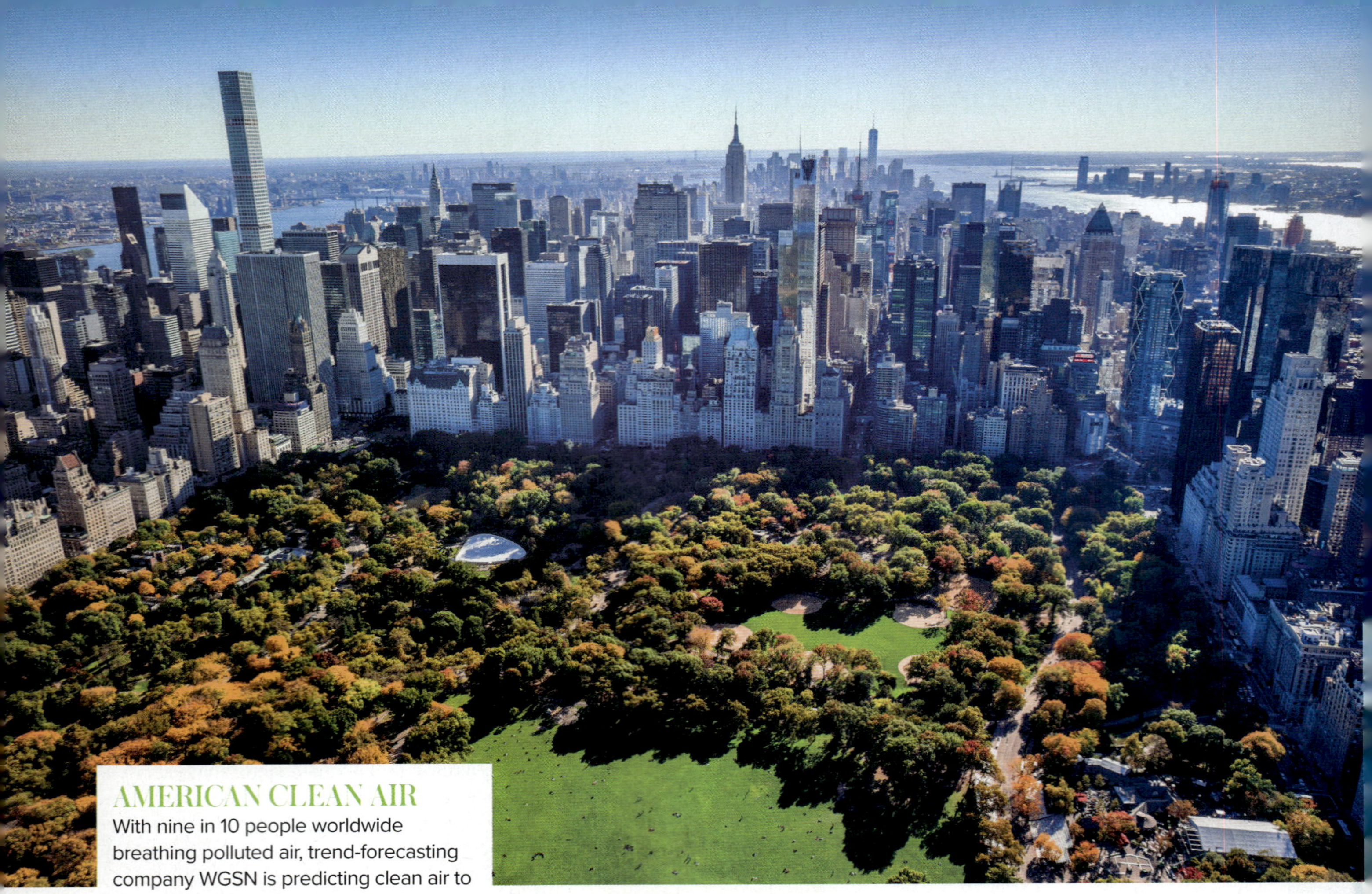

AMERICAN CLEAN AIR

With nine in 10 people worldwide breathing polluted air, trend-forecasting company WGSN is predicting clean air to become the latest wellness trend. However, it's not just outdoor activities that are leaving us at risk. Thanks to the recycled air and high levels of CO_2 in our gyms, our indoor fitness sessions may be threatening our wellbeing too.

The lack of ventilation also means there are particles entering the air from mats and bags that are being pummelled as people exercise, while heavier breathing through your mouth, rather than through your nose's filtering system, may be compromising your lungs' health.

The answer? In the US, clean-breathing gyms are on the rise. Studio 26 in New York City has two plant-adorned "living walls" installed inside, which release fresh air into their eco-friendly studios for a clean-breathing workout experience. And the additional advantage of the foliage releasing happy pheromones, means you'll get a post-training high too.

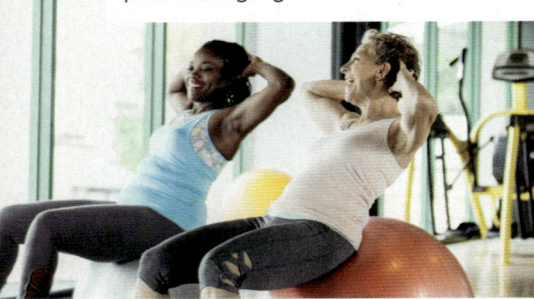

MEANWHILE THE BRITS ARE GETTING ON THEIR BIKES

In a bid to avoid transport delays and traffic congestion, the UK is lacing up its trainers and pounding the pavements to get to work.

"The rise of cycle commuting is well-documented, but lately Strava data has uncovered a meteoric rise in run commuting," explains Strava's UK country manager, Gareth Mills.

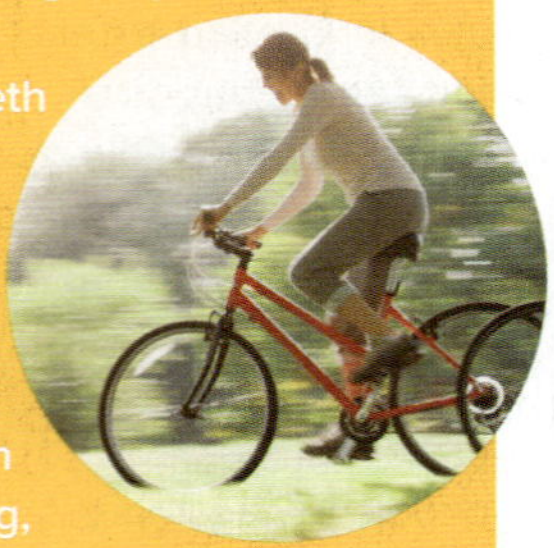

According to a report by Strava, the UK is the world leader in run commuting, which is up 56% from 2017. You'll not only save time – by 2020 it's predicted that average running speeds will overtake vehicle speeds in London – but you'll save money and get fit. It's an ideal way to fit in exercise around work, as well as carving out an uninterrupted mental space to prepare for work, or wind-down on the journey home.

INDIA'S LATEST MEDITATION TREND

Many centres in India offer sound healing as a holistic treatment to counter stress, stabilise blood pressure and boost the immune system. "Sound meditation has been practised for thousands of years, but has become a bit of an overnight sensation," says Leo Cosendai, author of the healing audiobook *Seven Days of Sound Meditation*.

The practice uses instruments in order to flood the body with vibrational sound, known as "sound bathing". The Siddha and Sound Spa programme at Svatma, a boutique hotel and spa in Tamil Nadu, India, offers a sound healing treatment inspired by a Veena, a traditional string Indian instrument. You lie on a bed of strings, which your therapist then plays. The 33 strings tally with the 33 vertebrae in the spine for an acoustic massage that induces a deep state of relaxation.

Another therapy making (sound) waves in the East, is gong meditation. "The frequencies and vibrations have various effects depending on the individual experiencing the sounds," says Leo. During a session, you lie down in a comfortable position on a mat, before your gong teacher begins to play. The sound energy from the gong vibrates

WORDS ELEANOR VOUSDEN **PHOTOGRAPHS** GETTY IMAGES, GETTY IMAGES/IMAGE SOURCE, GETTY IMAGES/ISTOCKPHOTO, GETTY IMAGES/TETRA IMAGES, GETTY IMAGES/VETTA, JUMP FOTOAGENTUR/KRISTIANE VEY

WELLNESS AROUND THE WORLD

the water in your body (of which 80% is water), sending vibrational waves that are felt from head to toe.

"It will give you an energising high, as if you've slept solidly for eight hours," says Leo. However, depending on the individual and their current emotional state, it could provoke a release of pent-up emotions – in some cases ending in a cathartic cry. Other benefits include heightened self-awareness, improved lateral thinking for problem-solving, and the ability to relax at will.

SWITZERLAND, HOME OF SOPHROLOGY

Mindfulness, meditation and yoga are now well-known practices, but sophrology, originating in Switzerland, is set to take centre stage. Sophrology is fundamentally "moving meditation" that is said to decrease stress and anxiety levels, as well as improve focus, sleep quality and mental wellbeing.

"The guided practice involves a combination of special and proven breathwork, relaxation, gentle body movements, meditation and visualisation techniques designed to bring you into the 'alpha brainwave' state – which boosts creativity and reduces depression," says Dominique Antiglio, sophrologist, founder of BeSophro, and author of *The Life-Changing Power of Sophrology*. In this meditative state, the body achieves full relaxation, yet the mind is clear and sharp. "Over time, particularly when you feel stressed, your mind and body will naturally trigger this response to bring you back to a calmer, more balanced state," she says. All it takes is just 10 minutes of practice each day.

THE "PUMP" SOPHROLOGY TECHNIQUE

When you're feeling stressed, Dominique recommends this soothing sophrology method…

1. Standing tall, let your arms fall straight alongside your body and clench your fists.
2. Now exhale through your mouth, then inhale through your nose and hold the breath. As you hold the breath, "pump" both your shoulders up and down until you need to exhale again.
3. As you exhale vigorously, relax your arms and hands completely, allowing all tension and tightness to drain simultaneously through the arms and hands.
4. Repeat these steps until you feel calm and rebalanced once more.

MINDFUL TRAVEL | 13

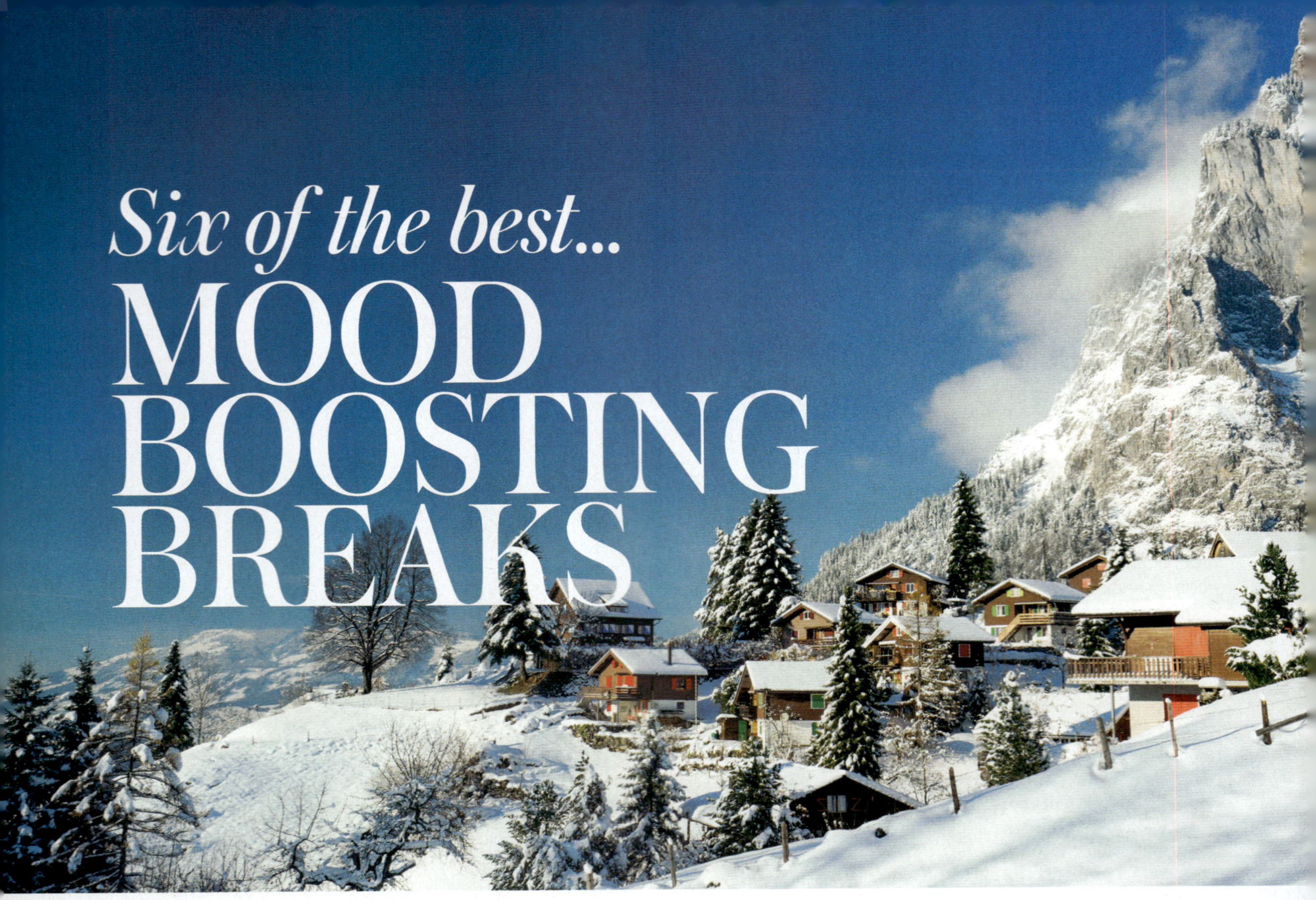

Six of the best... MOOD BOOSTING BREAKS

Whether you're thinking UK-based or abroad, weekend or week-long, booking one of these trips will put a well-earned smile on your face

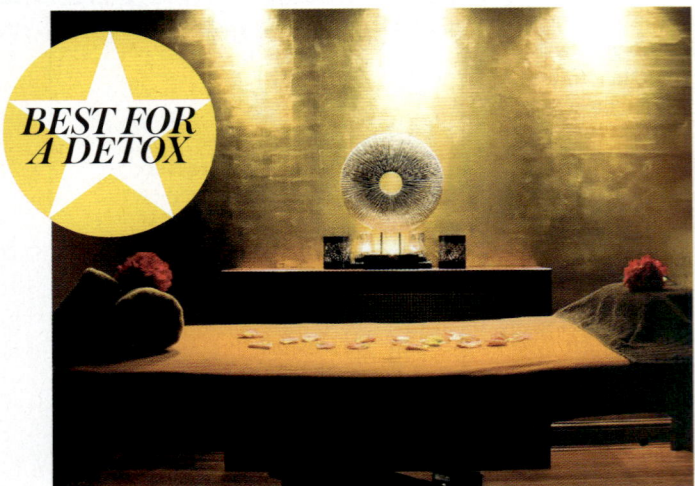

SIMPLY HEALING RETREAT, HORSHAM

A residential retreat, this focuses solely on your health and wellbeing. Delicious juices rid the body of toxins, helping with constipation, headaches, IBS, low energy and weight loss. The Simply Healing Juice Cleanse 5 Day Detox Plan includes a detox massage, detox foot spa and two sessions of colonic hydrotherapy among other treatments. You'll leave feeling like a whole new woman.

* **FIND OUT MORE Visit the website at simplyhealingcentre.com**

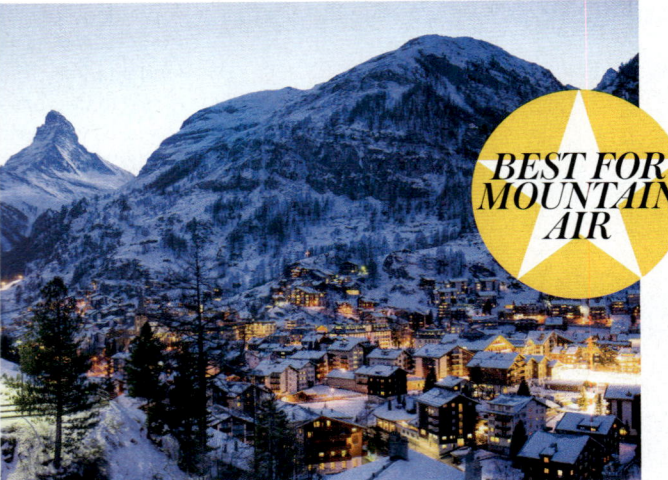

HARD ROCK HOTEL DAVOS, SWISS ALPS

Dubbed one of the healthiest places on earth, the Swiss Alps' mountain air promotes better breathing by giving your lungs a clean boost of oxygen. The Hard Rock Hotel Davos is home to the Rock Om programme – an in-room yoga experience that energises body and soul through the power of music. Plus, the hotel boasts a lavish wellness centre. Want to get outside? Davos is a ski resort, so there's a chance to get seriously active!

* **FIND OUT MORE Visit the website at hardrockhotels.com/davos**

COMPILED BY: LUCY GORNALL. PHOTOS: ALAMY, GETTY

MOOD-BOOSTING BREAKS

MIM IBIZA HOTEL AND O BEACH
Best for letting your hair down

Ibiza isn't just for the young crowd. In fact, you're only as young as you feel, we say! Stay at the adults-only MiM Ibiza Hotel, where poolside music is a given. Then spend your days at O Beach Ibiza, set around the beautiful S'Arenal waterfront on the west side of the island, where all the action is focused around a 600m2 swimming pool. Music and dancing are non-stop and the entertainment – think acrobatics and sky-shows – will have you hooked. Plus there are therapists on hand for an invigorating massage, should you need it.

✱ **FIND OUT MORE** Visit the website athotelmimibiza.com and obeachibiza.com

4 MASONS COURT, STRATFORD-UPON-AVON
Best for literary lovers

The birthplace of one of the world's most famous and important literary figures, the Midlands market town of Stratford-upon-Avon is steeped in history, and the legacy of its most famous son, William Shakespeare, is apparent throughout. Catch some of h eing performed at the Royal Shakespeare Theatre; visit the cottage where his wife, Anne Hathaway, used to live before they married; and explore the impressive timber-framed house where the Bard himself was born. Stay at the 15th-century Grade II-listed 4 Masons Court, the oldest house in Stratford-upon-Avon.

✱ **FIND OUT MORE** Visit the website at sykescottages.co.uk

PORT LYMPNE RESERVE, KENT
Best for nature

If you want guaranteed sightings of some of the world's rarest species, head to the Port Lympne conservation reserve, home to a range of animals who stay there with a view to being returned to the wild. You'll see tigers, giraffes, gorillas and more, cared for by The Aspinall Foundation. The reserve has a range of accommodation, from four-star lodges to camping, so you can take a well-earned break on the wild side!

✱ **FIND OUT MORE** Visit the website at aspinallfoundation.org/port-lympne

TRUE BLUE BAY RESORT, GRENADA
Best for chocolate lovers

Fan of the sweet stuff? Chocolate treatments are the order of the day at this Caribbean resort, from facials to body wraps and even a cocoa-infused bath. The spa uses organic Grenadian chocolate, which is brimming with antioxidants. True Blue Bay also has four swimming pools, a fitness centre and offers a range of complimentary water sports, so if you do end up over-indulging in the resort's decadent delights, you can salve your conscience with a workout.

✱ **FIND OUT MORE** Visit the website at truebluebay.com

PERFECT FOR Countryside tranquillity and farm-to-table food

BOHO CHIC IN IBIZA

The White Isle may be known for its dance-til-dawn culture, but that's only a small part of what Ibiza has to offer. Away from the crowds there's a quiet energy that island residents recognise as almost spiritual. Enter Cas Gasi, an ancient finca dating back to 1880. With 450 olive, almond and fig trees, and organic vegetable plots, this white farmhouse offers a peaceful paradise serving up delicious seasonal menus right in the middle of Ibiza. Here it's about unwinding — head out to the yoga deck for a complimentary wake-up session, have a sunset Swedish massage as the sky changes colour, or find a cosy nook amid the mismatched vintage armchairs for a moment of solitude. Just a 30-minute drive from the airport, this boho-chic hotel is the ideal retreat to reboot and fully recharge.
* **FIND OUT MORE** Visit the website at casgasi.com

10 feel-good GETAWAYS

For a holiday that'll leave you rejuvenated, relaxed and ready to face anything, take your pick from our favourite retreats
Words by **Geoffrey Palmer, Jane Druker, Katy Holland, Miranda McMinn and Zoe West**

10 FEEL-GOOD GETAWAYS

UNWIND IN ANTIGUA

PERFECT FOR Ultimate indulgence by the sea

It's hard to imagine a finer place to relax than Antigua in the Caribbean. On this beautiful and friendly island is the glamorous beachside Curtain Bluff resort.

As you drive through the gates you move from real life into what seems like another world, where your every whim is catered for under the palm trees by an army of smiling staff. The resort is set on its own private promontory, with two exclusive beaches plus a swimming pool, immaculate facilities, beachfront rooms and two excellent restaurants. But most importantly, absolutely everything is included, from breakfast through lunch and dinner, to even the cheeky piña colada you suddenly decide you need while relaxing on your waterside recliner in mid-afternoon.

* **FIND OUT MORE** Visit the website at curtainbluff.com

Curtain Bluff provides luxury in a truly tropical setting

WILDLIFE IN MYANMAR

PERFECT FOR An exotic but eco-friendly holiday

The remote Myeik Archipelago is a string of 800 tiny jungle-wrapped islands scattered over the Andaman Sea, just off the eastern coast of Myanmar. It has only recently opened up to tourism, and is still under strict regulation – its first hotel, Wa Ale, is a luxurious, intimate eco-tourism project that donates a chunk of its revenues to local initiatives, such as sea turtle hatcheries, coral protection and local ntrepreneurship. Set in the heart of the Lampi Marine National Park, Wa Ale's accommodation consists of sumptuous solar-powered tented beach villas and wooden treetop homes. New for this year is an exclusive beach house.

Expect to get up close and personal with rare and wonderful wildlife, including giant flying squirrels, gibbons, macaques and pangolins, as well as whale sharks, dolphins and manta rays.

* **FIND OUT MORE** Visit the website at waaleresort.com »

Enjoy stunning views from the tented beach villas at Wa Ale

PERFECT FOR Discovering an ancient winemaking region

FOOD AND WINE TASTING IN CRETE

Perched on the shore of Crete's eastern coast, the five-star Blue Palace Resort is a whitewashed modern resort sculpted into the hillside with panoramic coastal views. Bungalows, suites and private villas are dotted around the gardens, most with infinity pools. This hotel is in the heart of one of the world's oldest wine making regions, and it's a great place to discover your inner sommelier. You'll find a host of wine experiences run by the hotel, including tasting sessions aboard its traditional caique fishing boat and cellar tours. This is a good base for exploring ancient villages, as well as the Palace of Knossos. Visit the Minoan wine press at Vathypetro or stroll to the village of Plaka with its cheery meze bars.

✴ **FIND OUT MORE** Visit the website at bluepalace.gr

RELAXATION IN THE WEST COUNTRY

PERFECT FOR Luxurious recharging from your busy life

Lucknam Park sits in stunning, rolling Wiltshire countryside. It's an authentic country house, and the vibe is luxurious and elegant but always friendly. The grounds are vast (500 acres) and the overall feel is like being a guest in a Jane Austen novel – what could be more restful than taking a turn around the gardens, reading in the library and later having drinks in the beautifully appointed drawing room? Unlike Jane Austen heroines, though, you can also take a cycle ride, do yoga and Pilates, and visit the award-winning spa. Restaurant Hywel Jones is grand and befits its Michelin star status. We had divine lobster, melting pork belly, copious amuse-bouches and petits fours – and even the cheeseboard is served on a trolley! This is a place for real luxury and relaxation. So go on, treat yourself.

✴ **FIND OUT MORE** Visit the website at prideofbritainhotels.com

The hotel is near Bath, but it's a destination in itself

10 FEEL-GOOD GETAWAYS

WALK THE SCOTTISH COAST

Discover some of Britain's most glorious beaches on a walking holiday along the rugged Scottish coast. The week-long walk goes from the Forth Estuary to the medieval city of St Andrews, along the Fife Coastal Path. The 63-mile route takes in hidden caves, quaint fishing villages and a succession of historic sites, including the castles at Aberdour and Wemyss and Kincraig Hill. The tour, organised by walking specialists Celtic Trails, also features boat trips to the isles of Inchcolm and May, where puffins peek out from their grassy burrows. There's lots more thrilling wildlife to spot along the way, including dolphins, as well as spectacular wildflowers in spring.

PERFECT FOR
Revelling in history and wildlife

✱ **FIND OUT MORE**
Visit the website at celtictrailswalkingholidays.co.uk >>

DISCOVER SECRET PROVENCE

PERFECT FOR Stunning views and unspoilt countryside

With dramatic landscapes, rolling hills and the scent of lavender and flowers filling the air, it's no wonder that Provence has long been a favourite destination for holidaymakers looking for joyous escapes – and there are still some secret spots to discover if you venture off the beaten track. Make your way to the spectacular Cévennes National Park, with its steep river gorges and ancient villages, and you'll get a taste of unspoilt rural France at its finest.

Book in to La Maison Papillons, a restored Provencal farmhouse complete with lavender-fringed pool and views over the Cévennes. Surrounded by vineyards and orchards, with free-roaming chickens and flower-filled gardens, this chic hilltop B&B is a great spot for some serious R&R. Nearby you'll find the Gorges de l'Ardèche, an impressive canyon with sandy beaches and a huge natural limestone arch spanning the river. Cycle to local vineyards, visit markets and head to the beautiful medieval village of La Roque-sur-Cèze, with its cobbled streets. La Maison Papillons is part of i-escape's Secret Collection for 2020.

✻ FIND OUT MORE Visit the website at i-escape.com/la-maison-papillons

10 FEEL-GOOD GETAWAYS

There's a well-stocked library here too

PERFECT FOR Working on your creative inspiration

WRITE IN RURAL YORKSHIRE

Unleash your inner muse on a residential writers' retreat, set in an 18th-century mill owner's house in West Yorkshire, which once belonged to English poet Ted Hughes. Lumb Bank is hidden away in 20 acres of woodlands with valley views, perfect for getting the creative juices flowing. There's a host of writing courses available, with sessions led by well-known writers and evening readings in a relaxed setting.
✱ **FIND OUT MORE** Visit the website at arvon.org

A COSY COTTAGE IN COUNTY FERMANAGH

County Fermanagh, aka Northern Ireland's Lake District, is one of the most scenic counties of Northern Ireland. The Crom Estate nature reserve, on the shores of Upper Lough Erne, boasts wonderful scenery and teems with wildlife all year around. Stay at one of seven National Trust cottages gathered around a courtyard, all with open fires and comfy furnishings. Walks around the reserve provide plenty of opportunities for winter wildlife spotting; look out for pine martens, fallow deer and red squirrels.
✱ **FIND OUT MORE** Visit the website at nationaltrust.org.uk/holidays

PERFECT FOR A weekend of wildlife spotting

Stay in a courtyard cottage on a nature reserve

Learn how to live in the moment and get back to being your best self

PERFECT FOR A bespoke health and wellbeing boost

A FITNESS RETREAT IN KENT

Whether you need to kick-start your exercise routine or recharge your wellbeing batteries, Stede Court Private Fitness Retreat, set in beautiful countryside in Biddenden in Kent, is the place to do it. Owner Kathryn Freeland, described as 'the world's most sought-after trainer', has created an idyllic spot to find some me time. With outdoor fitness training for all abilities, healthy food, sauna and swimming pond, here you'll find peace and calm.
✱ **FIND OUT MORE** Visit the website at stedecourtprivatefitnessretreat.co.uk

MINDFUL TRAVEL | 21

EAT WELL *around the* WORLD!

Heading away this summer? Sampling the local produce could have more benefits than you think…

Want some good news? Even a two-week holiday can be enough time for your new surroundings to have a positive effect on your health. "When we're on holiday, we tend to be less busy and stressed, and take more time to eat," says nutritionist Sophie Thurner (sophiethurnernutrition.com). "We celebrate our food more, tasting different dishes and trying new flavours. Not only will this diversify our microbes, it will increase our consciousness around food, which has been shown to increase satiety and lead to less overeating." Here's what to try…

🇫🇷 FRANCE

"While full-fat cream, butter, bread, tarts and croissants are the norm, behaviour around food is what makes the diet special," says Thurner. "The big difference is the smaller portion sizes and the speed of eating. Because the French celebrate their food, they eat much more slowly, which allows fullness signals to reach the brain before overeating." The French eat twice as much cheese as we do, but research shows that eating cheese means you produce higher levels of butyric acid, which boosts your metabolism.

EAT WELL AROUND THE WORLD

SPAIN, ITALY, PORTUGAL AND GREECE

"The Mediterranean diet is based on plant-based foods, such as fibre-rich wholegrains (breads, pasta, couscous), nutrient-rich fruits and vegetables (artichokes, spinach, clementines), beans, seeds, fish, healthy fats (like polyphenol-rich olive oil), and less meat and dairy. It even includes some alcohol," says Thurner. The combination seems to be key for fighting disease and longevity, with Southern Italy having a high number of centenarians. Research in the Netherlands found that it could help cut the risk of a certain type of breast cancer by 40%. Plus, a study in New York indicated it could preserve brain cells as we age, while a group of international scientists say it can help keep depression at bay.

SWEDEN, NORWAY, FINLAND, ICELAND AND DENMARK

The typical Nordic diet includes hardly anything processed, but plenty of seafood, seeds (chia, pumpkin, sesame) and pulses (beans, lentils, peas). This could be why obesity levels in Sweden and Norway are around half of those in the UK. "There are many reasons why Scandinavians are not fat, and diet is one of the main ones," says Trine Hahnemann, author of *Copenhagen Food* (Quadrille, £25). "A Nordic diet is also an excellent source of omega-3 fatty acids," adds Thurner. "Plus, Nordic bread is often wholegrain sourdough. This is usually fermented, making it great for blood glucose levels."

Anyone for haggis?
The meaty Scottish dish might not be to everyone's taste, but it's packed with magnesium, iron, selenium, calcium, zinc and copper – great for bone health and regulating hormone levels.

 NEW ZEALAND

New Zealand is the source of manuka honey, great for fighting colds and soothing inflammation. "Raw honey has antibacterial properties, but these are easily destroyed by heat and light," says Thurner. "However, manuka honey contains a natural compound that maintains its antibacterial properties."

INDIA

"The Indian diet has a strong focus on vegetables, legumes and wholegrains," says Thurner. "It also offers a vast variety of flavours – thalis are made up of sweet, salt, bitter, sour and spicy. This is great for the gut, as it promotes a variety of microbes." Capsaicin from chillies can help ease headaches. "Spices can have antioxidant, blood cholesterol and glucose-regulating properties," says Thurner.

 JAPAN

Scientists in Tokyo found that a Japanese diet – low in fat, high in grains (rice), vegetables (such as mushrooms and seaweed), bean products, tofu, miso and fish – can reduce early death by 15%. "Meals consist of small plates of different dishes," says Thurner. "This increases the variety of food taken in a meal. The Japanese diet is associated with a lower risk of cardiovascular disease, cancer, diabetes and Alzheimer's."

Washing down sushi with green tea adds even more benefits. "Matcha and gyokuro are shade grown, so the plant pumps lots of L-theanine and chlorophyll into the upper leaves," says tea expert Johnathan Benson from T2. "L-theanine brings about a state of alertness, while taking green tea with food enables the body to absorb more vitamins."

The best of the rest...

✢ **AUSTRALIA** Try the versatile fish barramundi. Mild in flavour, it has half the calories of salmon, but is packed with the same omega-3 fatty acids. Visiting Sydney? Go for oysters. They're high in protein to help you feel fuller for longer, plus a great source of zinc and iron.

✢ **AMERICA** The USA might be famed for cholesterol-clogging burgers, but there are plenty of healthy options – just watch your portion sizes. Visit San Francisco for sourdough bread, which is lower GI than usual breads. Pick wild Alaskan salmon (fewer calories than farmed varieties), for bone-protecting selenium. In Florida? Key lime pie can help digestion.

✢ **SOUTHEAST ASIA** Broths, either bone broth soup, vegetable or miso, will fill you up and are packed with beneficial herbs and spices. Tom yum (Thailand) contains lemongrass, which relieves bloating, while pho (Vietnam) has calcium, phosphorus and magnesium for bone health.

Wales
Who needs caviar, when the next best thing is Welsh laverbread? Made with seaweed, this delicacy is packed with nutrients. "It contains iodine, an integral part in regulating thyroid hormones," reveals Thurner.

WORDS: FAYE M SMITH. PHOTOGRAPHS: GETTY IMAGES

Hidden CITY GEMS

Discover these celebrated spots and fabulous finds in four popular European destinations

HIDDEN CITY GEMS

AMSTERDAM
Follow the locals to discover this super-chilled, stylish city.

Amsterdam is a city that venerates art, architecture and design. The atmosphere is extremely relaxed and pleasant, the culture mind-blowing, and its buildings and canals beautiful enough to rival Venice.

There's less pollution than in UK cities – it's all about bikes and trams. There are 881,000 bikes for 811,185 residents, and 58% of them cycle daily – be careful when crossing the road!

A good way to find your bearings is with a canal trip. There are scores on offer, such as 'The Tourist', a gem of a 1920s 'salon boat' owned by the Pulitzer Amsterdam luxury hotel. This wooden beauty boasts a bar, floral arrangements worthy of a Dutch flower painting, red leather banquettes and, best of all (when I went), Captain Tony, who leads a 75-minute round trip of the city's waterways pointing out sites of interest (the houses of Rembrandt and Anne Frank, for example), in perfect English with a gorgeous Dutch accent. A must. Real Amsterdammers hang out in the cool hipster end of town — Jordaan and the Western Canal/9 Streets area, all ultra-tasteful health food cafés, and art and design shops. This is an endlessly attractive place to compare the subtle differences in the main canals, the red and yellow roses growing up the fronts of houses, the lavish window boxes, the houseboats and gabled 17th-century terraces. Definitely worth a trip is Ons' Lieve Heer op Solder. This translates as 'Our Lord In The Attic' and is a clandestine Catholic church set in the roof of a perfectly preserved 17th-century home, which feels a bit like entering one of the paintings by a Dutch Old Master, with black-and-white floors, narrow staircases and beds in cupboards. Be warned — it is situated in the heart of the infamous red-light district, which is itself worth a quick look if you have the stomach for reefer smoke and sex shops.

For the city's major art treasures, visit the Van Gogh Museum — a fascinating exploration of the artist through a chronological display of paintings and letters. Among more than 200 artworks are the famous Sunflowers, The Bedroom and The Harvest. Queues (as for the Anne Frank museum) are huge, so pre-book and arrive as early as possible. Slightly less crowded, though equally stuffed with extraordinary artworks is the Rijksmuseum, a huge national gallery where every corridor leads you to a yet more recognisable paintings — Vermeer's The Milkmaid, Rembrandt's The Night Watch — you get the idea. The museum is epic and the side galleries featuring special exhibits are another treat.

If you go to Holland, you must eat two things. The first is an Indonesian meal — as compulsory to the Dutch as a curry would be to a Brit. Try Puri Mas, a first-floor restaurant near Leidseplein, where the waiting staff wear traditional batik and they play calming jazz. Rijsttafel is a traditional Indonesian meal featuring multiple dishes of mouth-watering satay, gado-gado, noodles drenched in coconut, peanut sauce and fragrant spices.

The other must is a pancake house. The Pancake Bakery on Prinsengracht is prettily situated canalside and while the menu features modern twists, such as caprese, you really can't go wrong with the old Dutch classic (apple, bacon and syrup).

Dutch cheese, gin and tulip bulbs are the clichés, but shop in the Art Deli (art-deli.com) or Droog (hoteldroog.com) for a great gift range to impress folks back home. »

✣ For flight options, see skyscanner.net, or take the train via Brussels; eurostar.com
✣ For more information see iamsterdam.com and holland.com

The ornate Ons' Lieve Heer op Solder museum

Clockwise from left: Droog; Dutch cheese; exploring by bike; A touring canal boat; The Pancake Bakery

Clockwise, from top: Mandarin Oriental terraces, with a view of the Eiffel Tower; Beaupassage; the Marais district; Buly

PARIS

Enjoy fashion, food and French chic.

The Paris Fashion Week crowds may have disappeared, but for style and luxury this city has year-round appeal, with top-notch art, fashion, cuisine and entertainment at every turn.

You can't beat simple pleasures such as strolling along its elegant, tree-lined boulevards, or watching the sun set over the River Seine – but there are tucked-away gems you also need to know about.

On Rue Saint-Honoré, the Mandarin Oriental hotel is the epitome of refinement, with its own secret garden in the heart of the city, luxurious rooms and a superb spa. In its Michelin two-star restaurant, Sur Mesure, overseen by one of France's leading chefs, Thierry Marx, the dishes are as much about art as food.

What's more, the Mandarin Oriental has introduced a Shop Like A Parisian package with an insider's guide – The Parisienne's Notebook – co-curated with the city's iconic, online lifestyle magazine, Do it in Paris.

One of the latest lunch destinations is Beaupassage, in the heart of the 7th arrondissement, where the crème de la crème of the Parisian food scene have set up shop. Thierry Marx La Boulangerie on Rue de Laborde makes for an inexpensive stop-off, with delicious savouries that fuse oriental and French flavours and irresistible sweet fancies.

If you've never visited a fashion atelier, nearby Maison Rabih Kayrouz, tucked away in a courtyard, is the place to try. Featuring a workshop and boutique, you can glimpse the team making the Lebanese designer's stunning clothes – from gorgeous draped dresses and blouses to chic, structured designs.

And if you're going to splash some cash on style, a visit to a bijou perfumier is a must. Situated in the trendy Le Marais district, with its medieval network of lanes, Buly is filled with divine scents. Dark, polished wood, marble counters and fragrances based on Mexican tuberose, Peruvian heliotrope or Scottish lichen make for a truly memorable experience. The Marais is also home to a marvel of renaissance design – Musée Carnavalet on Rue des Francs Bourgeois. It's the place to discover the history of Paris, as told through art, design and architecture – and has reopened after a mammoth three-year renovation project.

A 10-minute walk away in Rue Froissart, you'll find one the area's newest eateries, Malro. Contemporary with a buzzy vibe and delicious Mediterranean-inspired dishes, it's the perfect way to round off a day's exploring.

✛ **The Mandarin Oriental Shop Like A Parisian package, €1,185 for 2 per night; mandarinoriental.com**
✛ **For general info on Paris, visit en.parisinfo.com**

HIDDEN CITY GEMS

EDINBURGH
Be inspired in Scotland's capital.

There's always something special to discover in Edinburgh, whether it's the historic Old Town and Castle, the elegant New Town (actually not so new, as it was built in the 18th century), the world-class museums, or simply the stunning street vistas and open spaces. A good place to start is the famous Princes Street. Be sure to admire the Scott Monument, and call into the Scottish National Gallery, where you'll see the much-loved 'Skating Minister' — a painting that seems to embody the calm, unruffled character of the courteous Edinburgh Scots.

And if you're looking for a quality venue to dine, head to Ondine, an excellent seafood restaurant in the Old Town. While walking there from the New Town, literature fans should look out for Deacon Brodie's Tavern at 435 Lawnmarket. Brodie was one of the real-life inspirations for Robert Louis Stevenson's Dr Jekyll and Mr Hyde.

After a busy day, try the Printing Press Bar & Kitchen on George Street. And why not finish the night with music at The Jazz Bar on Chambers Street?

On Sunday, you may want to do more sightseeing. Keen readers should enjoy The Writers' Museum in the Old Town, located in Lady Stair's House, built in 1622. It's packed with portraits, books and belongings of famous Scottish writers Robert Burns, Sir Walter Scott and Robert Louis Stevenson.

Another area worth exploring is the old Leith docks area and The Shore, now an attractive waterside hang-out. Afterwards, for a real treat, go for drinks and dinner at the nearby Lighthouse Bar on the floating ship, Fingal. Both hugely romantic and Art Deco stylish, Fingal has sumptuous leather sofas and marble-topped tables.

To round off the weekend, head to the Scottish National Portrait Gallery on Queen Street. Just sitting in the Great Hall of this neo-Gothic palace, with its frieze of the great and good of Scotland, is an experience in itself.

> ✈ Fly to Edinburgh Airport, then take the tram into town. Or go by rail on the LNER to Edinburgh Waverley station; edinburgh.org

Clockwise, from left: Fingal floating hotel; seafood at Ondine; the Leith docks area

VENICE
A hideaway island that boasts a cooking academy.

The lure of Venice's historic centre is irresistible, but there are little-known delights in La Serenissima too. One such is Venice's 'youngest' island, Isola delle Rose, a lush, green retreat that sits on the edge of the lagoon, backed by the deep blue Adriatic Sea. It's now the home of the luxurious JW Marriott Venice Resort & Spa, which you can get to via a James Bond-style 20-minute speedboat shuttle from Marco Polo Airport (around €150), or the tourist water bus (two hours).

This hotel is the perfect destination for combining culture with some R&R — it has a stunning outdoor rooftop pool (pictured below), with incredible views of Venice and St Mark's Square. And if that doesn't lower your cortisol levels, the fabulous spa certainly will.

But the hotel's gem is its very own Sapori Cooking Academy, which is set amid beautiful gardens complete with a kitchen garden and orchards.

Classes with expert chefs will take your culinary skills to a whole new level (from €80pp). Learn how to make Italian biscuits with a top Italian pastry chef, try your hand at making fresh pasta, Venetian-style tapas, pizzas or focaccia, or book the 'Authentic Venice' course, which involves a trip to the famous Rialto Market to stock up on local produce before returning to the Academy to learn how to turn them into mouth-watering Italian dishes. Return home and you'll be able to recreate la dolce vita in your very own kitchen.

> ✈ 3 nights at JW Marriott Venice, from £845pp, based on two sharing B&B, including return flights with easyJet from London Gatwick and private transfers; destinology.co.uk

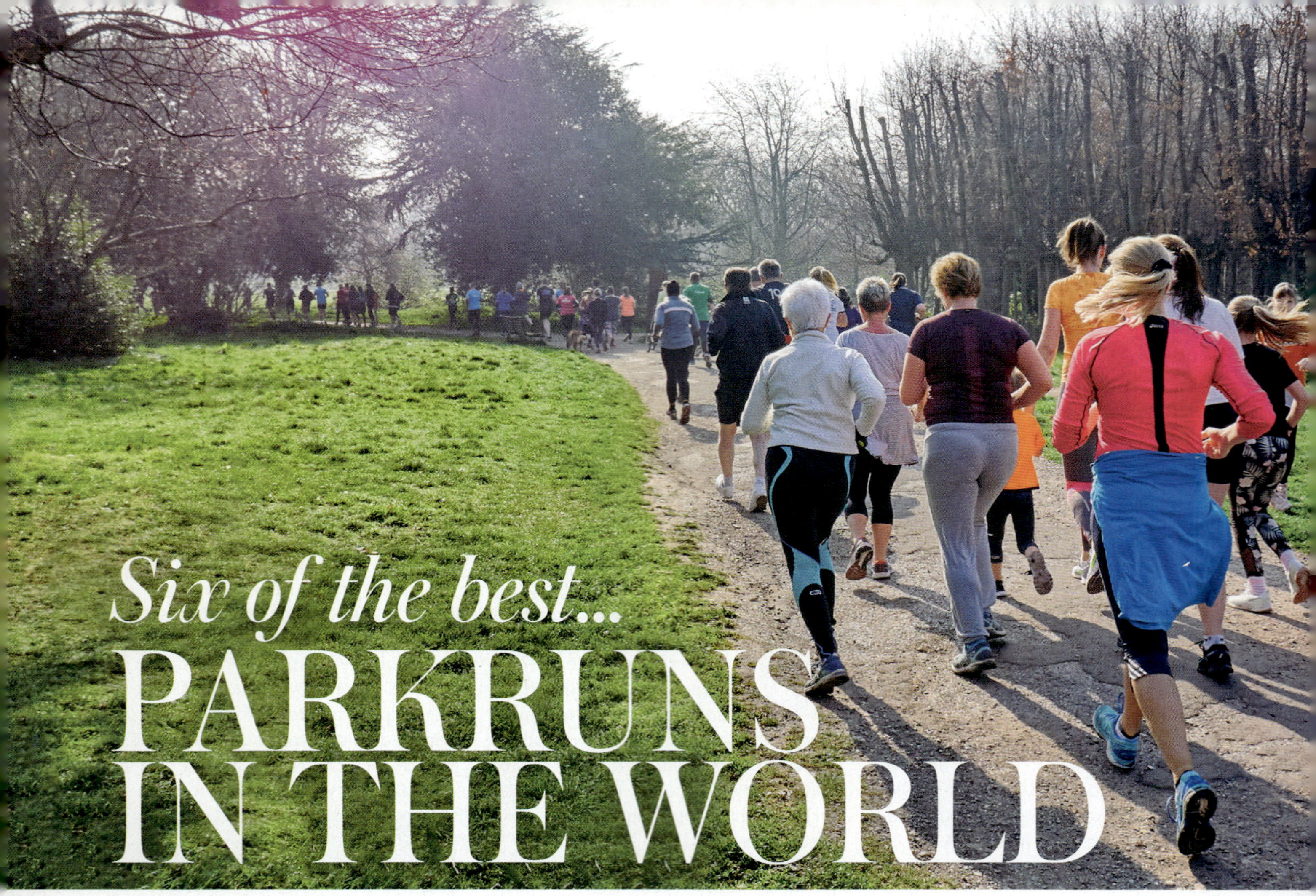

Six of the best... PARKRUNS IN THE WORLD

In 15 years, parkrun has grown from one event in London to 1,800 free, weekly, timed 5km runs around the world. Here are our favourites...

BEST FOR WHERE IT ALL STARTED

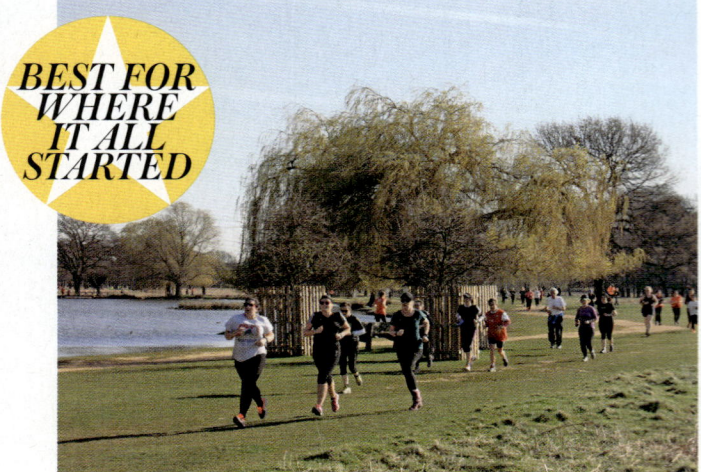

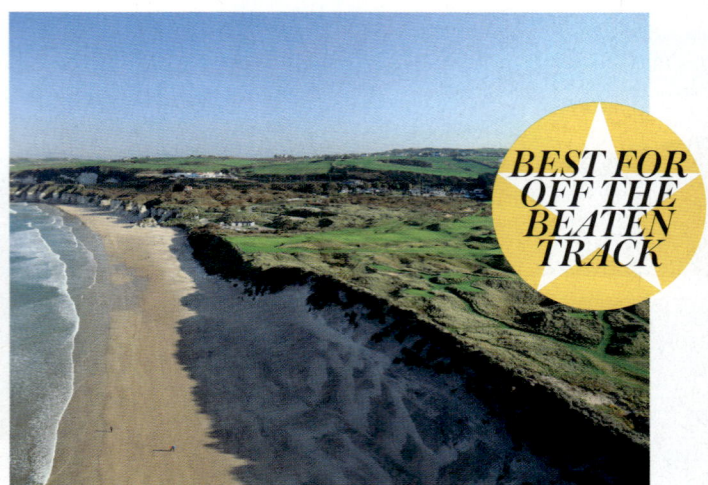

BUSHY PARK, RICHMOND, LONDON

Before 2004, no one had heard of parkruns. But thanks to Paul Sinton-Hewitt CBE, on 2 October that year, the royal park held its first free run event under its original name, Bushy Park Time Trial. Starting with just 13 runners on its first day, the part-grassy, part-footpath route now holds the UK's record number of entrants for a parkrun with 2,011 on Christmas Day 2018. It's pretty fast and flat, and the scenery doesn't disappoint either. Originally established as a hunting ground by Henry VIII, you may spot a deer or two.

BEST FOR OFF THE BEATEN TRACK

PORTRUSH, NORTHERN IRELAND

When we say off the beaten track, we mean it. That's because there's not a footpath, track or even a park in sight – just sand. When it started in September 2012, it was the first beach parkrun in the world run entirely on sand – and it's now still the only one in the UK. Bounding down a beach may be a bit of a killer workout for your calves, but it certainly offers a unique experience, completing 5km with the backdrop of waves crashing against the shore and a view of Dunluce Castle and the Giant's Causeway. Trainers optional (seriously!).

MOOD-BOOSTING BREAKS

BEST FOR THE WILDLIFE

KANGAROO ISLAND, AUSTRALIA

It's there in the title – wildlife is built right in. Travelling down under this year? Head to Australia's third-largest island for a 5km adventure trail. This jaw-dropping out-and-back course follows footpaths along the coastline, so you should be able to hop to the finish line in pretty good time, as long as you don't get distracted by the wallabies, koalas, seals and kangaroos. Just allow time to get there, as it's a 45-minute ferry ride from the mainland port of Cape Jervis.

BEST FOR A CHALLENGE

ASHTON COURT, BRISTOL, ENGLAND

If you're a bit of a whizz when it comes to a 5km, this might be just the challenge you're looking for. With a 2.5km uphill start, this will really get those legs and lungs working hard (and there's no shame in walking the super-steep bits!). You'll be rewarded at the turning point with fantastic views over Bristol and the promise of a downhill stretch back to the finish. The route runs along tarmac and stone/gravel paths, making the course suitable all year round.

Why not set yourself the challenge of becoming an alphabeteer? This is where you tick off parkruns for each letter of the alphabet...

BEST FOR SIGHTSEEING

CRISSY FIELD, SAN FRANCISCO, CALIFORNIA

They say one of the best ways to see a city is to lace up your trainers and get moving. So if you want to tick off the sights of San Fran, then this is one not to be missed. It's no wonder the parkrun team have seen an increase in tourists from the UK, Australia and beyond taking part. On just the first mile, runners will be up close and personal with San Francisco Bay and the Golden Gate Bridge, while on the return leg, there are striking views across to Alcatraz, as well as the San Francisco skyline.

BEST FOR EARLY RISERS

EAST COAST, SINGAPORE

It already boasts the title as the first country in south-east Asia to host a parkrun, and it could win an award as one of the steamiest. The humidity in Singapore can reach 96%, thanks to its frequent rainfall, high temperatures and close proximity to the sea, which is why this parkrun starts 90 minutes earlier than others around the globe, with kick-off at a supposedly cooler 7.30am. Despite the early start, you'll undoubtedly still work up a sweat as you weave your way along the coast, dodging dog walkers and Buddhist monks.

Yes, you CAN AFFORD a holiday home!

Achieving the two-home dream is more affordable than you think. Andréa Childs finds out how from the experts – and readers who've already done it…

It takes just a glimpse of sun for most of us to begin the "What if and where… Would we, could we…" conversation. What if we had a holiday place that we could whizz off to at the weekend? Where would we buy, here in the UK or a cheap-flight bolthole abroad? Would we make the most of it – and could we ever afford it?

Depending on who you talk to, having a holiday home is either the new property investment of choice, with returns of up to 12% a year. Or the next financial – and ethical – black hole, thanks to increased stamp duty and pricing out local residents. (St Ives and Gwynedd have imposed restrictions on second-home ownership and other councils are set to follow.) The consensus is that a holiday let, which the owner uses but also rents out (covering costs plus bringing visitors and income to the local economy), is better than a second home, which spends most of the time empty.

And it may be more affordable than you think. Read on for the expert guide to making your two-home dream come true…

BUYING IN THE UK

Affordable hotspots

In the UK, most holiday homeowners live an average of 120 miles from their second property. To find a place that's affordable but still attractive to renters, search out areas adjacent to better-known spots. Liz Daniels, founder of breconcottages.com, says, "The Brecon Beacons isn't Pembrokeshire, so we don't command the same sort of rental. But the area is popular for its footpaths and rivers for canoeing and kayaking, and it's an easy drive from Cardiff, Birmingham, Oxford and London."

"Paignton in South Devon is less expensive than nearby Torquay but has access to all the same amenities," says Luke McCaughan from bluechipowners.co.uk. He also tips Weymouth and Portland in Dorset as affordable investments that appeal to Londoners looking for a weekend getaway. And then there's the east of the country.

"The coastline of Lincolnshire is breathtakingly beautiful, and when you compare it with eye-wateringly

Search out areas adjacent to better-known spots

AFFORDING A HOLIDAY HOME

Melanie now runs a yoga retreat from her Andalucian home (left)

'We've managed to buy a beautiful house in Spain by renting in the UK'

Melanie Melvin, 51, and her husband Craig, 49, sold their Brighton home, found a nearby rental, and used their remaining equity to buy a traditional stone house in Andalucia, Spain. They have two teenage children.

Having a house in Spain is a huge privilege but it came about through difficult circumstances. I was working as a business coach as well as a yoga teacher, and Craig had a marketing consultancy, but after the financial crash in 2008, getting work was tough. We were struggling to pay our mortgage and building up debts.

Four years ago, we sold our house and paid off everything we owed. We decided to rent a house in Brighton, where our children go to school, and invest the £75,000 we had left in an old stone house in Andalucia.

We already loved the area, and were friends with the owners of the nearby B&B. They told us when the house came on the market and we bought it as a getaway – both Craig and I are writers (his first novel is being published soon), so it's a place to come with our laptops and write in peace.

Then the B&B owners said they had a group of women coming to stay and asked if I could run yoga sessions for them. Our house is small but it has a huge terrace that's perfect for yoga; a friend gave us 50 workout mats for free; and suddenly I was running a retreat! [In 2019, I hosted] three holidays here, with guests staying at the B&B but coming here for yoga, meditation and swimming.

We've found a balance between running a business and having a second home. We visit as a family three times a year, checking out the cheapest flights to Malaga airport on skyscanner.net. Life here is relaxed and affordable; you can buy a coffee for €1 in a café and just talk; no one's staring at their phone. We go to the beach or walk in the mountains. We always feel better physically and emotionally when we spend time here, but we love Brighton, too. We love to go away and we love to come back; it feels like this was meant to be.
lunarlemonproductions.com/retreats

expensive Norfolk, it becomes even more attractive," says Linda Jeffcoat of property search site stacks.co.uk

Clever property picks
Once you've found where you want to buy, it's time to think about the type of property. In the UK, quirky spaces – shepherd's huts, houseboats, even treehouses – are cheaper than a cottage but can command a premium for renting out. And when it comes to bricks and mortar, smaller can be better. "A property that sleeps two or four is less limited than one that sleeps six to eight, which is often difficult to fill," explains Liz Daniels. A shed to store bikes and good parking so you don't have far to carry suitcases are plus points. You'll also want a shop nearby. "Even if it's the sort attached to a garage, as long as it sells the essentials," says Linda Jeffcoat. "A pub is an obvious amenity too. If there's a farm shop and café as well, that's perfect."

And remember that while a remote cottage may seem a bargain, its location may come with hidden costs. "If your second home is in the middle of nowhere, you may struggle to find local people to carry out cleaning and maintenance," says Kate Faulkner of propertychecklists.co.uk

Getting there
Anyone who has started their summer "escape" by sitting in a traffic jam knows how crucial holiday travel can be. "If you're looking at clogged motorways on a Friday and Sunday night, you need to think twice about escaping for a short weekend," says Linda Jeffcoat.

Do your sums
New tax benefits make investing in a holiday home an attractive option, but for it to qualify as one, you will need to rent it out commercially for short lets for at least 105 days a year. Do that and you can claim allowances for furniture and fixtures, and count earnings as income for pension purposes.

It's not all money for nothing, though. Second homes attract additional stamp duty rates and may be subject to higher council tax. If you need a mortgage, you'll typically need a deposit of 25% of the property value. Seek advice from an independent mortgage broker since there is a smaller choice of lenders offering holiday-let mortgages. Furness Building Society specialises in this area. >>

Rent your property for 105 days a year to qualify for tax benefits

MINDFUL TRAVEL | 31

BUYING ABROAD

Affordable hotspots

Again, pick up-and-coming or overlooked locations. "Greece is experiencing a tourism boom but property prices in Athens are still 40% below their 2008 peak," says George Kachmazov of overseas property broker tranio.com. In France, Fleur Buckley from frenchentree.com cites Limousin – known as "the French Lake District" – as her in-the-know tip. "Farmhouses in need of renovation with acres of land can be snapped up for €80,000, or pick up a large barn for €20,000," she says.

Overseas, the essentials remain the same. "Supermarkets, restaurants and pharmacies are all important," advises Julian Walker of property broker spotblue.com. "And look out for a local doctor's surgery, particularly if you plan to retire to the property."

Getting there

Forward-planning is key. "Be savvy with booking flights. Low-cost carriers like easyJet release tickets in waves throughout the year, often up to 10 months in advance. The best deals are usually found as soon as they drop, but flights are also dependent on demand so look out for flash sales," says travel journalist Tracey Davies.

Do your sums

Seek expert advice as each country's mortgage criteria, inheritance and tax rules are different. "Even if you're a cash buyer, a mortgage may still be the best option as it offsets fluctuations in exchange rates and means you know exactly what you're paying each month," advises Fleur Buckley.

Look for companies that specialise in overseas property purchases, which can highlight common pitfalls such as not having the proper permits for renovations. Shows such as aplaceinthesun.com, theoverseaspropertyshow.com and propertyinvestor.co.uk are a good place to find property, legal and financial advice on turning that two-home dream into a reality.

Plan your visits. Booking flights months in advance will get the best deal

Susan eventually wants to live in France full-time

'It's not just a holiday house, it's a home'

Susan Eyres, 55, and her husband Richard Pulford, 50, live in Bowdon, Cheshire, and bought a three-bedroom house on France's Cote d'Azur in 2011.

I've been coming to France every summer since I was two as my grandfather had a motorboat moored on the Mediterranean coast. After he died, my dad bought a boat and carried on the tradition, eventually finding a spot in a harbour in Sanary-sur-Mer, a lovely Provençal fishing port about an hour from Marseille. Later, Richard and I decided to buy a more permanent place in the village. We used savings for the deposit, and pay our mortgage in euros.

At home in Cheshire, we're walking distance from restaurants, shops and the tram to Manchester. We wanted our place in France to be just as well connected – when you're coming for a weekend, you don't want to spend hours waiting for a cab or getting to the beach. I run Gateway Gallery, a contemporary art gallery in Hale, Cheshire, and will escape to France for long weekends a few times a year. I can catch a flight from Manchester at 11am and I'll be sipping a drink on the terrace just a few hours later. If we're coming for longer, say at Christmas, Richard and I pack up the car – and our dog – and do the 16-hour drive down through France.

Sanary-sur-Mer is a place to relax and escape. We do a lot of lunching out, day trips and relaxing by the pool. We also let it out occasionally, as empty second homes can kill a village and we don't want to harm Sanary – I've been to St Tropez at Christmas and it's dead. Renting also covers some of the costs of maintaining the property. For us, though, this isn't an investment; it's a lifestyle. We've already decided we'd eventually prefer to sell our Bowdon house and live here full-time instead.

AFFORDING A HOLIDAY HOME

'We love our romantic beach-hut bolthole'

Trish and Matthew Kelvie own a luxury beach hut in Shaldon, South Devon. They have two teenage daughters and live in West Hythe, Kent.

Matthew and I had our first date in Shaldon 27 years ago and I also have happy memories of holidaying here as a child. When we saw the beach hut pop up on the TV show *George Clarke's Amazing Spaces* four years ago, we immediately wanted to find out more. It was an emotional response but also a practical one.

Matthew had recently sold a business so we had money to invest. I was a full-time mum at the time and looking for a way to earn an income to build up a pension. The hut seemed the perfect solution, and since you can also sleep there – not the case in most beach huts – it would give us a place to escape to at the weekends.

Matthew and Trish often rent out their hut

Although it's only small, our hut is a luxury build, with granite work surfaces in the kitchen, a stone-tiled shower and bifold doors leading on to the terrace and the sandy beach. It cost us £207,000 and we paid in cash, as we wouldn't have been able to get a mortgage on it. We haven't recouped that cost yet, but it is rented out for around 320 nights a year, so the investment is making more than if the money was just sitting in the bank.

It's a four-hour drive away, so we rely on a local cleaner and caretaker to maintain it for us.

We've learnt the best times of day to travel, so even if we're here for a night, it feels like a holiday. I love sitting on the terrace watching the waves and the lights twinkling across the bay. As our girls grow up I'm looking forward to the time when Matthew and I can stay longer and really make the most of this place. It's romantic; a place for the two of us to enjoy together.
shaldonbeachhut.co.uk

THREE GREAT HOMES ABROAD

1 STONE HOUSE WITH SEA VIEWS IN GREECE, €270,000
This two-story villa on the island of Thasos has sea and mountain views, a swimming pool and a private garden including a barbecue area. See **tranio.com**

2 BUILT-TO-ORDER VILLA IN SPAIN, €281,672
This detached villa in Guardamar, Alicante, has three bedrooms, two bathrooms and a shared pool, with a Blue Flag beach just a 10-minute drive away. See **propertyandspain.co.uk**

3 HOUSE AND BARN IN WESTERN FRANCE, €149,330
Tucked down a quiet lane in the village of Nere in Poitou-Charentes on the Atlantic coast, this three-bedroom house is within walking distance of a bar/restaurant. See **frenchestateagents.com**

FAR, FAR away

Feast your eyes on the stunning scenery of these dream destinations, which combine the fascination of new cultures with glorious landscapes

MAURITIUS

A wellness resort on a tropical island? It's the perfect place to refresh.

'Mauritius was made first and then heaven, heaven being copied after Mauritius.' So wrote Mark Twain – and he was right. This island jewel in the Indian Ocean sits 20 degrees south of the equator, and its glorious weather makes it a year-round paradise. The south is densely tropical, with palms, ancient banyan trees, vines and flowers to enjoy along winding coastal roads. Set amid the 2,500-acre Heritage resort, Hotel Le Telfair maintains a charming 'village' feel, with no buildings over two storeys high. Relax and refresh by the pool, with its ocean view, and watch the kite surfers move across the glittering water. Take a stroll up the beach, which is beautifully wild and untamed, yet still picture perfect. Stop by the Coco Shack, where delicious fresh coconuts (added rum punch is optional) are served up daily.

FAR, FAR AWAY

The stunning island of Mauritius offers sandy white beaches and crystal-clear waters

Feeling adventurous? The resort's gentle estuary is the ideal place to learn to paddleboard, or try your hand at laser sailing and windsurfing. A snorkelling trip reveals rainbow shoals of fish, as well as sea turtles, or you can simply relax and enjoy the view from a glass-bottom boat trip.

The resort focuses on wellness, and offers everything from a tranquil massage in the Seven Colours spa, to two blissful hours of sunset yoga, set in the impressive manicured grounds of the Heritage Le Château, where you can also enjoy divine food. The island has cultural and culinary influences from Africa, Europe, China and India, and with a choice of 12 restaurants at the hotel, it's hard to pick a highlight, but Gin'ja is especially beautiful at night, when its darkly lit wooden structure glows against the white sand beach. Sip a sundowner champagne cocktail by the firepit or try pan-Asian food, flambéed rum seafood, a superb sushi selection, dim sum and teppanyaki. Beyond the resort, Le Morne offers bareback horse riding on the beach with Haras du Morne (haras-du-morne.business.site), or swimming with dolphins with Karlos Excursions (karlosexcursions.com). Rum fans will enjoy the guided tour at Rhumerie de Chamarel (rhumeriedechamarel.com), or you can visit for a cocktail or afternoon tea in the pretty surroundings.

And don't miss the lunar-like spectacle of Seven Coloured Earth, a volcanic geopark of vividly coloured dunes – red, brown, violet, green, blue, purple and yellow – dating back 600 million years.

Or quad bike your way around Casela Nature Park, where you can encounter zebras, ostriches and rare white rhinos. For a panoramic view, launch yourself off Thrill Mountain for the 40m-canyon swing or zip line across breathtaking valleys. Nerves of steel optional. >>

TO BOOK

∴ Rooms at the Heritage Le Telfair are available in a choice of B&B, half-board, or all-inclusive options; heritageresorts.mu
∴ Fly direct with Air Mauritius; airmauritius.com

MINDFUL TRAVEL | 35

SRI LANKA

This beautiful island is rightly famed for its wildlife, glorious beaches and cultural heritage.

Whiling away the days on a private beach, reading in the shade of a coconut tree and watching fishermen bringing in the catch of the day for the Salt restaurant... it's a recipe for sheer bliss, and makes the Shinagawa Beach Hotel in Balapitiya the perfect place to begin a holiday in Sri Lanka.

When you're ready, head to Dambulla to discover the island's wonders in the Cultural Triangle. A visit to the Dambulla Cave Temple is a humbling experience. Each of its five caves has beautifully painted ceilings and is filled with statues of the Buddha. It's a phenomenal sight.

Next, climb Sigiriya, known locally as Lion Rock because a colossal brick lion once guarded the entrance. At 656ft high, it dominates the skyline for miles, so you do need to be fairly fit and definitely not afraid of heights!

A short drive from Dambulla, the Minneriya National Park is one of the best places to spot wild elephants – and who could visit Sri Lanka without seeing these wonderful creatures?

The dry season from April to October is one of the best times to visit, as elephants gather at waterholes to feed and bathe. Flocks of birds, such as cormorants, painted storks, herons and pelicans, fish in the shallow waters too.

Another drive takes you to Galle, on Sri Lanka's southwestern tip. It's a Unesco World Heritage Site, with imposing Dutch-colonial buildings, ancient mosques, churches and museums. Wandering its lanes, you'll pass stylish cafes, quirky boutiques and impeccably restored hotels.

Check into Le Grand, a contemporary waterfront hotel tucked away from the hustle and bustle, but only minutes away from the walled Galle Fort. Its spacious rooms all have terraces with stunning ocean views, and the boutique hotel maintains a personal feel.

A Sri Lankan experience has it all, but it's made all the more special by the friendly people you meet along the way. It is truly an island to love.

"Lion Rock dominates the skyline for miles around"

FAR, FAR AWAY

Traditional fishing and busy beaches of Galle; see elephants in Minneriya National Park; and gorgeous temples in Dambulla

Experience the beautiful Colombo skyline; see leopards in Yala National Park

VIETNAM

Discover the wonders of the East Sea as you explore the delights of Central Vietnam.

With jungle-clad mountains, long stretches of sparkling coastline and Unesco World Heritage Sites, Central Vietnam is the perfect destination to reconnect with nature and experience a new culture. Discover its unmissable destinations and luxurious resorts.

The ancient riverside town of Hoi An is uniquely charming. Stroll through the virtually traffic-free streets of the former trading port, where traditional buildings stand with French colonial architecture, a Japanese covered bridge and ornate Chinese temples.

Foodies will delight in the succulent street food – the Hoi An noodle special is cao lau, served with crispy pork and herbs. The atmosphere grows dreamier by night, when the river glows in the light of paper lanterns and floating candles. Buy handmade crafts from artisan markets, or custom dresses and suits from affordable, high-quality tailors.

Just an hour from Hoi An is the My Son Sanctuary, a Unesco Heritage Site that breathes tranquillity and mystery. Circled by verdant mountains, the sanctuary is home to an extensive collection of Cham remains, created by My Son civilisations from the 4th to 13th centuries. Wander through the lush jungle valley and discover dramatic temples. Devoted to Cham kings and

FAR, FAR AWAY

"The river glows in the soft light of hundreds of paper lanterns"

Enjoy a boat ride in Hue; the stunning nightlife of Hoi An; visit the ruins of My Son; and learn to fish at local fishing villages

Hindu deities, elaborate symbols are carved onto temple walls.

Hue, the former capital and home of emperors past, boasts historic grandeur. Its formidable fortress, enclosed by stone walls, reveals temples, moats and palaces. Meandering through the city is the Perfume River, so named for its aroma of flowers. Stroll or cycle along its banks, or cruise through on a boat tour.

Within easy reach of all Central Vietnam's historic gems is the Laguna Lăng Cô resort. Nestled between forests of the Truong Son mountains and waters of the East Sea, the resort has two unrivalled hotels to offer.

With spacious suites, Angsana makes a great family getaway. Its design balances modern elements and traditional decor, with sea-view rooms. On-site restaurant the Rice Bowl cooks up local delicacies, while beachside Moomba is a hotspot for succulent seafood. Fine wines and whiskey are on the menu at Rice Bar, where expert chefs prepare fresh sushi. With discovery and adventure at the heart, get active on hikes, golf courses and private pools, or recharge at the spa.

For blissful peace and ultimate luxury, head to Banyan Tree. This sanctuary for the senses is the perfect hideaway for couples. Secluded villas come complete with infinity pools, offering vistas of serene lagoons and the glittering East Sea. Dining options include unbeatable Thai cuisine at Saffron, and Vietnamese classics at The Water Court. Sip cocktails at Thu Quan bar, or opt for a 'floating breakfast' in your private pool. Asian therapies are available from the spa, where a range of luxurious treatments focus on harmony of the mind, spirit and body.

TO BOOK
✣ Fly into Da Nang Airport and you'll be within an hour's drive of Lang Co Resort.
✣ banyantree.com

Six of the best... WATERSIDE BREAKS

Whether you want a travel adventure or a relaxing weekend away, there's always something incredibly soothing about staying by the water...

BEST FOR BEACHSIDE BLISS

TENBY, WALES
Sand stretching for miles, blue sea and skies... you could be forgiven for thinking this is a spot in the Mediterranean. But look closer – this is Tenby on the south-west coast of Wales. The small harbour town sits on a hilltop above the Pembrokeshire coastline, where waves foam along the beach and you can stroll along the sands. Alternatively, take a boat trip from the harbour to get really close to the water, and bounce across the waves, the spray hitting your face.
* **FIND OUT MORE** Visit the website at tenbyvisitorguide.co.uk

BEST FOR CRUISING

KERALA, SOUTHERN INDIA
Houseboats in Kerala meander slowly past rice fields and, as they're skippered, you can just relax as you listen to the rush of the water by the bow and wait for sunset. Best avoided in monsoon season (June-August), it's warm all year round, but there's always the possibility of rain! The 11-day Tropical Kerala package from Meraki Travel (merakitravel.co.uk) includes an overnight stay on a houseboat as well as a visit to a spice plantation.
* **FIND OUT MORE** Visit the website at keralatourism.org

WATERSIDE BREAKS

BEST FOR CRYSTAL CLEAR PARADISE

MALDIVES, INDIAN OCEAN

The water in the Maldives is so crystal-clear, it's like its been Photoshopped – you can see to the bottom of the ocean. This is ideal snorkelling territory, and you may find yourself swimming with breathtaking manta rays and whale sharks. Home to around 5% of the Earth's reefs, the Maldives is a once-in-a-lifetime wonder that has to be seen to really be believed! The best way to visit is via an all-inclusive deal. A particularly luxurious option would be staying in an overwater pool suite on a full-board basis at the Amari Havodda Maldives resort.

✱ FIND OUT MORE Visit the website at maldives.com

BEST FOR ICY FUN

ANTARCTICA, SOUTHERN CHILE AND ARGENTINA

With icebergs floating around you, this is pure escapism. The wildlife here is mesmerising – you can spot seals and whales in the water and albatrosses soaring above you. Penguins live here in huge colonies, too. Summer is December to February, when the average temperature ranges between -10C and -30C. You fly into Puenta Arenas in southern Chile (from London with two stops) then go on by boat as part of a chartered tour.

✱ FIND OUT MORE Visit the website at discoveringantarctica.org.uk

BEST FOR LAKESIDE RELAXING

GRASMERE, LAKE DISTRICT

Smaller than Windermere, Grasmere was home to the poet Wordsworth and you can visit his home here. In spring, a stroll along the lakeside may reward you with the sight of 'a host of golden daffodils', such as those that inspired his famous poem. The beautiful and dramatic landscapes would inspire anyone! Enjoy a bird's-eye view of this vast expanse of calming water by climbing one of the surrounding fells – although you should prepare to get rained on. There are also picturesque waterfalls nearby when you take lakeside walks.

✱ FIND OUT MORE Visit the website at visitcumbria.com

BEST FOR ALPINE GLACIERS

THE FRENCH ALPS

You might associate them with snow, but in summer the French Alps are peppered with glacial lakes and forceful rivers, shining like gemstones with their icy, blue-green colour. The winter skiing resort of Chamonix near Mont Blanc gives way to wonderful hiking country in summer and allows access to the impressive Mer de Glace (sea of ice), while down in the valley near the town of Bourg-Saint-Maurice you can experience the thrill of rafting on the waters of the Isère river.

✱ FIND OUT MORE Visit the website at savoie-mont-blanc.com

We're living the MAMMA MIA DREAM!

We speak to three readers who've upped sticks and moved to an island paradise

LIVING THE MAMMA MIA DREAM

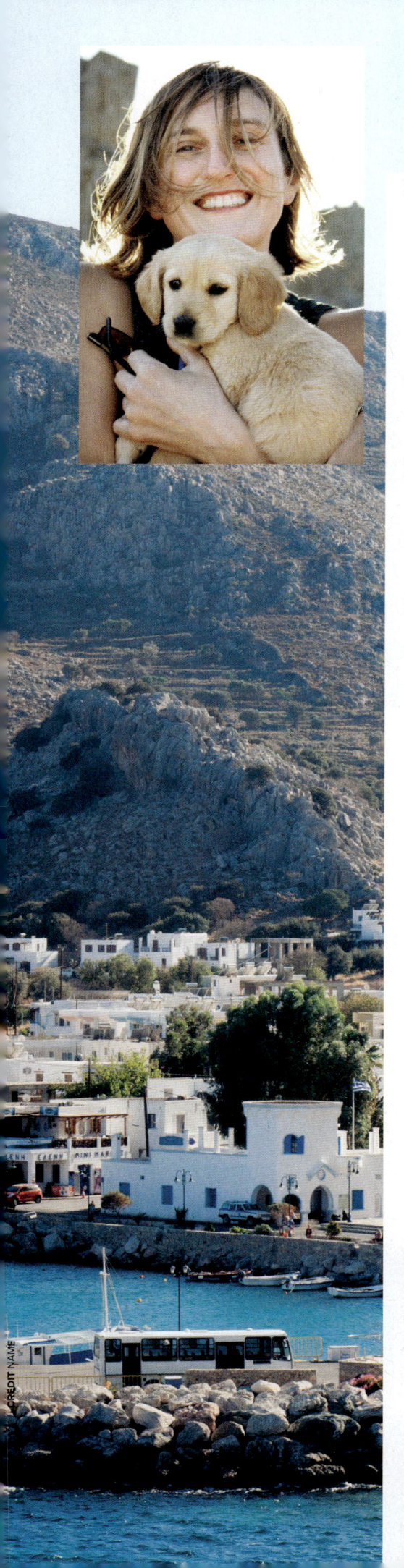

THE GREEK ISLAND
'I can lie in bed and hear the waves'

Jennifer Barclay moved to Tilos, a tiny Greek island, in 2011 where she now writes and edits books.

Shortly after my 40th birthday, I went through a difficult period after a relationship I'd been in ended suddenly. When the plans we'd had went out the window, I realised I wasn't completely happy with the life I had. Now that I only had myself to think about, I needed to work out what I really wanted in order to make myself happy.

The idea of moving to Greece had been planted in my mind a long time ago. I'd had a love affair with the country that had started when I was a child growing up in Yorkshire, and we spent many of our family holidays in Greece. I did Ancient Greek O and A levels, and after studying English at Oxford, decided to live in Athens for a year to teach English. Over the years, I kept revisiting the country.

On the eve of my 40th birthday, I decided now was the time to try living on a Greek island. I'd lived abroad for most of my adult life, spending several years in Canada and France, and had travelled for long periods, so moving abroad was not daunting. I knew I wanted somewhere very "Greek". Tilos has no airport and there isn't a ferry every day – it was perfect! I loved the peace and quiet, the mountains and beaches, and the friendly people.

Initially, I decided to give myself a month on Tilos to see if it was possible to work remotely. I was editorial director of a publishers based in Chichester and my boss kindly allowed me to go, and it worked well for the first couple of years until I decided to go freelance and start my own business. I moved permanently in 2011, and have rented several different houses – I now live in a house by the sea where I can hear the waves. Living with lower overheads has allowed me to do more of the things I love such as writing. My typical day involves a morning of serious work, then going for a long walk with my dog, Lisa, usually with a wild beach at the end of it. Although I like spending lots of time alone, I have plenty of friends, a mix of locals and expats from various countries. The population of the island is only about 300 in winter so, as you can imagine, you get to know everyone.

I'm working on becoming fluent in Greek though I'm not there yet, and I like to get involved in the local community. One winter I taught English to local children, and it was a wonderful way to get to know the parents.

> "The entire village pulled together to look for my lost house keys!"

So many people tell me how they'd love to do what I've done, but this isn't a life for everyone – it isn't the same as life in the UK certainly. Often things don't work properly, so you must go with the flow. There's a good community spirit, too, and people always try to help out – I once lost my house keys and the entire village pulled together to look for them!

After all the tourists go home at the end of the summer, I love it because I've got the island all to myself again.

✢ *An Octopus in My Ouzo: Loving Life on a Greek Island* by Jennifer Barclay is out now (Summersdale) >>

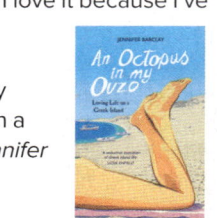

The seaview from Jennifer's apartment and, right, with one of the 300 locals who live on the island

THE CARIBBEAN
'Even a volcano couldn't wreck our paradise!'

Sarah Dickinson lives on the Caribbean island of Montserrat with her husband, John. She has two sons and four grandchildren. The moment I step outside our villa, I'm almost overwhelmed by our beautiful surroundings. The ocean stretches to my right, our infinity pool and orchard lie straight ahead, the sun climbs over the mountains to my left, and I'm more in love with Montserrat than I was when we first arrived in 1974.

Earlier that year, my husband John and I were on a summer holiday in France. Our trip almost ended in tragedy when the car I was driving spun out of control and hit a tree. John managed to get me out before it exploded. When something so dramatic occurs, it forces you to revaluate your life.

To cheer ourselves up later that year we headed to the West Indies on holiday, ending up on the little island of Montserrat. The island took our breath away. And the people! They love to laugh, they're incredibly generous and they have a great turn of phrase – "enjoy the balance of your day" is one I seem to have adopted. We vowed to come back as soon as possible. John is an architect and his dream was to build villas on the island. Having something so ambitious to focus on certainly helped in the healing process following the accident. We eventually found the perfect place, Isles Bay Plantation, and remortgaged everything we had to pay for it. Work started in 1989, and we'd managed to fund the building of the first four villas – we were aiming for nine – before hitting the first major hiccup when Hurricane Hugo devastated the island.

But this was nothing compared to what happened next. On 18 July 1995, Montserrat's Soufriere Hills volcano erupted for the first time in 400 years, shooting rocks, ash and gas into the air.

A state of emergency was declared, and the island's population of 11,000 people sank to 4,000. Our villas were safe because they are about 5km from the volcano but economically it was devastating for us – and everyone else on the island. We had to work 24/7 to juggle building work, loan repayments and our life at home back in the UK where our kids were still at school.

Between 1995 and 2010 the volcano erupted five more times, although it's behaved very well since then. I'm actually quite fond of this volcano now! But I have no regrets – we still haven't broken even though we have just started on phase two at Isles Bay Plantation. We've had the most incredible adventure living on this island.

✢ Plenty Mango, Postcards from the Caribbean *by Sarah Dickinson (Tamarind Press, Amazon, £12.99)* >>

Sarah and John (above) enjoy the adventure of living on this island

LIVING THE MAMMA MIA DREAM

IBIZA

'Ibiza is actually a really spiritual place'

Wendy Buttery owns The Lotus Pad, a yoga retreat in Ibiza. She moved to the island in 2012 where she lives with her partner Neil, a chef, who provides the food for their guests.

The peace and quiet of our retreat never fails to calm me. The most noise you'll ever hear is the buzz of a tractor somewhere in the distance. At night we're enveloped in darkness and in the morning, when I step outside, the first thing I see is the beautiful lemon tree, the one I fell in love with the day I arrived here. Our nearest town, Santa Eularia, is about 15 minutes drive away, with stunning beaches about the same distance. I can't imagine living anywhere else.

I've always been an adventurer and in my twenties I was bitten by the travel bug. I took temping jobs so I could save up to go away again but, by the time I'd reached my thirties, I realised that I needed to do something more concrete. I didn't ever want children, and in some ways this gave me an enormous amount of freedom. I'd been learning yoga for a few years and thought it would be something I'd love to teach. I qualified when I was 38, then went to teach in Goa.

It's quite common for yoga teachers to spend the winter in Goa and then go over to Ibiza for the summer. Ibiza is seen by many as a party island but it's actually a very spiritual place. There's a whole hippy culture of people who came in the sixties from India, making their way overland through Afghanistan. Some of those characters are still around, and that's what makes the island so interesting.

I came to Ibiza for the first time in 2009, arriving with £500 to my name. I ended up teaching yoga for the summer, and returned the following year, which is when I met my partner Neil – he helped me put up the teepee that I was living in!

After a couple of years, we decided to set up our own affordable yoga retreat. Property goes quickly in Ibiza and we had someone searching for us as we were in Goa. The first time I saw the house was the day we were moving in. Luckily, I loved it.

We have a wonderful life here. During the winter, I study yoga books, do baking and gardening, and visit the beaches. I believe the universe supports the person who makes the leap; sometimes you have to leap before you know there is a net to catch you. But the net *is* there, you just don't always see it.
lotuspadyoga.com

> "The peace calms me – I can't imagine living elsewhere"

Wendy loves her new life in Ibiza

WORDS ALLY OLIVER **PHOTOGRAPHS** ALAMY, GETTY IMAGES

The island's capital, Ibiza Town

MINDFUL TRAVEL | 45

Making MEMORIES *that last a lifetime*

A holiday is the perfect time to create meaningful moments that you always remember

There's a reason our favourite memories tend to be sun-drenched, and often triggered by the sounds and smells of the season. "Summer is when we take holidays, and the break from our daily routine expands the space for fun, connection and play," says psychologist Karen Young. We have time to plan, recalling previous golden times and putting the elements in place to recreate them.

Read on for our expert mindful guide on how to make, and appreciate, memories you will cherish forever…

OUR EXPERTS

EMILY ESFAHANI SMITH is a positive psychologist and author of *The Power of Meaning* (Rider Books)

KAREN YOUNG is a psychologist and the founder of the popular website heysigmund.com

RACHEL MARTIN is a life coach, specialising in mentoring women (rachelmartinlifecoaching.com)

1 Make time for meaningful moments

Great memories won't happen if we don't make space for special things. "Our lives are bursting at the seams with to-do lists so it can help to investigate whether we're spending our time doing what we'll look back on fondly," says Rachel Martin. She suggests drawing a chart with five columns and five rows. At the top, write from left to right: Stop, Do Less Of, Keep Doing, Do More Of and Start. Then think about your life and fill in the boxes under the headings. "This can be a total eye-opener – it reveals the activities that no longer serve us, as well as those that have the potential to change how we spend our time."

2 Tell your own story

We all tell stories about ourselves; it's how we make sense of our life and give it meaning. "One way to turn an experience into a lasting memory is to ask yourself how you will describe it to others later," says Emily Esfahani Smith. She says this is also a way to pull out what it is about a memory that you savour, so you can recreate it. "One of my favourite memories is the walk I took with my husband on the morning of our wedding before the guests arrived. What made it so special was the quiet and the two of us alone, totally connected. I won't have that moment again, but I can design the elements that made it significant into future moments with my husband."

MAKING MEMORIES THAT LAST A LIFETIME

3. It really is the thought that counts

When we want to craft a memorable atmosphere, think less about the details and focus on the bigger picture. "If you're having a birthday picnic, knowing that the sandwiches taste great will make you happy in the moment, but it's the thoughtfulness you put into the event that gives it lasting meaning," says Esfahani Smith. Think who the picnic is for. Serving their favourite foods, playing games they love, or choosing a special place will give it more significance than the perfect chicken-avocado wrap.

4. Put away the tech

You'll realise how much more you see, hear and feel without technology. "We live life through a lens, and love to show our highlights on social media. But it isn't real and it leaves us in a state of disconnect," says Martin. If you're taking pictures, take just one; don't take 100 trying to get the perfect shot. "I've been guilty of this," admits Martin. "Then I tell myself that when I'm gone and my son is looking at those photos, he won't care how I look. He'll care that I was there and that we shared a wonderful moment together."

'Treasured memories don't always have to be from planned events'

5. Try something new

Memories are imprinted in different ways. "Doing something challenging or novel will release feel-good chemicals in the brain, which can add a sense of exhilaration or joy," says Young. These emotions help create enduring memories. It's why we remember our first date, when we passed our driving test or did something daring for charity.

'We rented the same holiday home for 30 years'

Sarah Lockett studies Garden Design and lives in Bideford, Devon, with her husband Jon and their three children.

When I was seven, my dad spotted a rambling house to rent in Croyde, Devon. It had eight bedrooms, an Aga and a path to the beach from a huge garden. Both he and my mum had spent their childhood holidays in Devon and wanted to give me and my brother that experience, along with our grandparents, aunts, uncles and cousins. There were around 25 of us in all. We enjoyed ourselves so much that we booked for the next summer, then the next.

Eventually we would rent the house for Easter and autumn half-term each year, too, and came back for 30 years before the lady who owned the house died and her family sold it on. Going back to the same place was key as it always felt like home.

The memories of those times have stayed with us all. They were proper old-fashioned holidays with picnics on the beach and rounders on the lawn. Us kids spent hours writing and rehearsing a show that we'd perform on the last night. The grannies would sit in the sun room knitting and doing crosswords. And we'd all gather in the evening to eat together.

The holidays clearly left their mark because, over the years, me, my brother, my parents, an aunt and a cousin have all moved to Devon. And recently my cousins have been talking about finding a new holiday house to stay in and giving our children the chance to make their own memories.

"The memories of those times have stayed with us all"

Croyde was the ideal setting for holidays with the extended family

7 Start a tradition

Repetition can also help our brain recall events. "Memories become hardwired through time and experience, as the more of something we do, the more connections are formed in our brain," says Young. This is why traditions are more likely to create enduring memories. So if you always have a family picnic on the first day of summer, you're more likely to remember it than if it's a one-off event. Holidays are a great time to forge new memories – especially when you create triggers that take your mind back to your trip at a later date. "We have a tradition that we collect a Christmas decoration from every place we go on holiday – which can be tricky in the middle of summer," says Young. "When we put up the Christmas tree, the holiday souvenirs prompt conversations that start with, 'Do you remember when… ?'" Another idea is to create a playlist for holidays or particular events, as music has a special way of bringing memories to life.

6 Cherish your keepsakes

Memory boxes, scrapbooks and photo albums can also trigger memories and evoke shared recollections that help them maintain significance. "For a college friend's birthday, a group of us made her a scrapbook of our favourite times together. It was an opportunity to reflect on our lives and the friendships we cherish," says Esfahani Smith.

8 Count your blessings

The most beautiful moments can come from being alone and finding meaning in simple things. "Doing things with others amplifies certain moments, but being mindful or grateful when we are on our own can also do this," says Young. Gratitude puts the focus on what we have, rather than what we don't. Keep a journal and note down three things you're grateful for each day. This helps embed these good things in your consciousness.

'I create a handmade birthday card for my daughter every year'

Angela Evans runs her own cleaning business. She lives with her partner Michael and their daughter, Jorja, for whom she makes cards, in Altrincham, Cheshire.

It started when Jorja was two; I thought it would be sweet to make her a birthday card instead of buying one. I made a train with a photo of different family members in each carriage and stuck it on the wall so she could see it when she came downstairs. She loved it. Before her birthday the following year, she asked me to make another.

Now it's turned into Jorja deciding the theme – we've had unicorns, fairies and aeroplanes. I'm not a natural crafter so it can take me a week to make the card, watching YouTube videos on papercraft and how-to-make pop-up cards when she's in bed. But however many presents she has, the card is the first thing Jorja looks for on her birthday, and seeing her face when she spots it is priceless.

We keep all the cards in a memory box, along with other treasures such as the notes Jorja writes to me, photos and her artworks. One year, we also kept a memory jar. Starting on New Year's Day, we wrote a note every time we went or did something special and put it in the jar. At the end of the year, we took them all out and read them. It's like a Facebook timeline but with real items in front of you. Each one triggers an emotion. It's not just what we did but who we were with, what we said and funny things that happened.

The memories that stay with you aren't always the ones you expect – we're just as likely to remember the slip-ups and surprises. But that just makes them even more special.

ON SALE NOW!

On your marks, get set... glow!

Disocover how to bring out your natural radiance today with our brand-new title, filled to the brim with expert advice & amazing recommendations!

Ordering is easy. Go online at:

WWW.MAGAZINESDIRECT.COM

Or get it from selected supermarkets & newsagents

BEAUTIFUL BRITAIN

52 Isles of wonder
Nothing beats the thrill of seeing British wildlife up close and personal

56 Why there's no place better than the British countryside in summer
For making happy memories and enjoying the good life

58 Literary landscapes
Britain's breathtaking locations are as diverse as the writers they inspired

64 Six of the best… UK walking hotspots
There's nowhere like the UK for a fantastic place to walk

66 Taking the waters
Enjoy some of the UK's most beautiful and inspiring wild waters

70 Six of the best… UK swim spots
Dive in and reap the benefits of taking a dip outdoors

72 It's a shore thing
Here's our celebration of some jaw-dropping coastlines

76 Treasure island
Precious British offshore delights just waiting to be discovered

72

64

58

MINDFUL TRAVEL | 51

Isles of WONDER

From beavers to bats, nothing beats the thrill of seeing British wildlife up close and personal. Read on for where to go – and what to see

1 RED SQUIRRELS in the Yorkshire Dales

Star attraction This native species is now rare in Britain, with only 161,000 left, but there is a thriving population in the Widdale Squirrel Reserve in the Dales.
Why go? Up-close views of the red squirrels who are surprisingly tolerant of people, according to Yorkshire Dales wildlife conservation officer Ian Court. "They've learnt you're not a threat and you don't disturb them," he says.
What else will I see? Badgers, hedgehogs, buzzards, bullfinches and even lizards.

2 BEAVERS in East Devon

Star attraction There are now 25 busy beavers in the River Otter near Otterton, where you can watch them build lodges for their kits.
Why go? Since the species has been extinct in the UK for centuries, beaver-watching is something of a novelty; in fact, no one is quite sure how they came back! Now they are, let's hope they stay! Says Steve Hussey, spokesman for the Devon Wildlife Trust: "If you spot them, you'll be one of the first people in England to see them in 400 years." To put that in context, he adds, "It would be the time of Shakespeare when beavers were last seen in Britain – and even then they would have been rare."
What else will I see? A stable otter population – hence the town's name – plus kingfishers, dippers and grey wagtails for birders to enjoy.

3 BOTTLENOSE DOLPHINS in Cardigan Bay

Star attraction The 230-strong population of bottlenose dolphins can be spotted from Newquay Headland, Llangrannog and Mwnt on the west coast of Wales. Or why not join researchers on a Dolphin Survey boat trip (dolphinsurveyboattrips.co.uk)?
Why go? The five-mile stretch of coastline from Newquay to Tresaith was named the UK's first Marine Heritage Coast "because of its unspoiled natural beauty and the variety of wildlife," says Steve Hartley, the founder of Cardigan Bay Marine Wildlife Centre.
What else will I see? Atlantic grey seals and harbour porpoise swim by the shore. And, if you're lucky, you could see leatherback turtles in summer.

ISLES OF WONDER

4 EAGLES on the Isle of Mull

Star attraction White-tailed and golden eagles are the most famous residents on Mull off the west coast of Scotland. These are two of the rarest species in the UK – there are only 120 pairs of white-tailed eagles in the country, for instance, but 20 pairs live here.
Why go? White-tailed and golden eagles are unrivalled in their majesty, according to wildlife guide Ewan Miles. "In terms of their beauty and stunning behaviour, they're an emblematic species, and iconic to great wild landscapes."
What else will I see? Eagles aren't the only birds on the block; hen harriers and puffins draw crowds. Plus there are otters, humpback whales and killer whales in surrounding waters. »

MINDFUL TRAVEL | 53

5 BLUE-EYED GOLDEN HARES
on Rathlin Island, Northern Ireland

Star attraction Irish hares leap through the country's hills and farmland but Rathlin Island is unique because it is the only place you can find a golden hare. This genetic anomaly is rare, and there's only a handful each season.
Why go? RSPB warden Liam McFaul says the golden hare is worth tracking down. "When you see one, it's just amazing. It just sticks out of the landscape like a big ginger cat with these lovely sky-blue eyes."
What else will I see? One of the largest seabird colonies in Europe. The West Light Seabird Centre is home to puffins, guillemots, kittiwakes, razorbills and fulmars. Visit in the summer before they migrate.

6 GREY SEALS
in Blakeney Point, Norfolk

Star attraction Atlantic grey seals can be found in the harbour here, and a boat trip is the perfect way to get close to the largest seal colony in England, where 2,700 pups were born last year.
Why go? According to Ajay Tegala, National Trust ranger and wildlife presenter, the seals are "full of character and you get fantastic views of them here, but the great thing about Blakeney Point is that it's a wild landscape. The wind shifts shingle across the beach, causing the shore to constantly change shape. It's ever-changing and unique."
What else will I see? Further out, in the shallow part of the sea called The Wash, there's a thriving population of common seals that migrate to the harbour in the summer. On the mainland, you can spot barn owls, geese in the winter months and crabs in the summer — families can go crabbing in the creek.

ISLES OF WONDER

7 BATS
in the Falls of Clyde

Star attraction Take an evening stroll and look for hundreds of bats flying overhead.
Why go? The reserve has spectacular waterfalls and wildlife walks. Ranger Laura Preston says, "The more people find out about bats, the more they like them."
What else will I see? Evening badger walks are popular, also expect to see dippers, otters, deer and kingfishers.

8 RED DEER
in the Forest of Dean, Gloucestershire

Star attraction See over 1,000 deer including Roe, Fallow and Muntjac.
Why go? The annual stag rut is awe-inspiring. "And the forest is absolutely beautiful," says Tim Davies, spokesman for Wye Valley and Forest of Dean Tourism.
What else will I see? Plenty of wild boar and free-roaming sheep.

9 OSPREYS
in Rutland

Star attraction Ospreys live in a nest in the western section of the 23-mile reservoir in Rutland Water. You can watch them from Waderscape Hide or via a live-stream video from their nest in the Lyndon Visitor Centre.
Why go? Rutland is the only osprey site in England – after being driven to extinction 150 years ago, they were reintroduced in the 1990s. "They're impressive to watch as they fish, hovering above the water before diving in feet-first," says Dale Martin at the Rutland Water Nature Reserve.
What else will I see? The trees on the 1,000-acre nature reserve are home to nightingales, black caps and distinctive warblers, such as the chiffchaff.

10 PUFFINS
in Anglesey

Star attraction Hundreds of puffins roost at South Stack Cliffs RSPB reserve on the north-west coast of Wales – and there are photo opportunities aplenty from Ellins Tower or from the steps to the lighthouse.
Why go? This is an Area of Outstanding Natural Beauty, says Martin Jefferies, visitor operations manager at South Stack Cliffs. "We're also part of the Anglesey Coastal Path, so it's brilliant for walkers. Not only that, the 300 hectares is home to the spatulate fleawort, a flower that doesn't grow anywhere else in the world."
What else will I see? Guillemots, razorbills and the chough, the rarest member of the crow family in Britain with a very distinctive call, which draws crowds to the seabird colony.

"Why there's no better place than the BRITISH countryside, in summer"

For making happy memories and enjoying the good life, there's nothing like a staycation, writes Miranda McMinn – rain clouds and all!

What's your definition of a perfect summer's day? Here's mine… walking down a shady footpath next to a stream, legs brushed by buttercups and cow parsley, avoiding nettles, and everywhere you look, soothing green. Emerging into a field, climbing a stile, dodging curious cows. Eventually finding a picturesque picnic spot by a shallow river and lying there all afternoon comparing the contrast of grass and sky, while ladybirds wander across the blanket, cabbage whites flutter around you, and blackbirds and thrushes form a chorus from the branches above. When it's too hot, paddling in the shallows. Or an early morning walk along a dyke, admiring the fields stretching for miles and the dew burning off the meadow grass in a misty haze, and finally saying, "It's actually so hot I might take my cardigan off." Then later, in the garden, among lavender bushes and furry bumble bees, having a glass of wine, and then another and another, until it turns suddenly cool, everyone realises they're completely drunk and you all have to go straight to bed!

Really, there's nothing as perfect as the British countryside in summer, is there?

THE BRITISH COUNTRYSIDE IN SUMMER

"But what about the weather?" says everyone. Well in my view it's the weather that makes it. Not just because, as a lady put it to me succinctly one rainy summer weekend in Wales, in her lilting accent, "If it didn't rain so much it wouldn't be so green, would it?" But because of the unpredictability it keeps us on our toes, makes us grateful.

Yes, we carry on our love affair with the Mediterranean – but we take it for granted that it will be hot, that lemons will hang from the trees and the bougainvillea will blind us with purple brilliance. If it ever turns cloudy, rainy or – God forbid – cold, we're so cross we almost ask for our money back.

> "Now one of the greatest joys of this stage in my life is realising that I can access the countryside all by myself"

Back in Blighty, meanwhile, the one thing that is never taken for granted is a warm, sunny day. I am increasingly obsessed with the countryside – and I'm hardly being original, since nearly six million of us watch *Countryfile*, not to mention *Coast*, *Escape to the Country* and so on.

For me though I feel that it's a hasty, snatched, last-minute romance – one that I have to throw myself into headlong because I've wasted so much time – as I have always lived in Zone 2 of the Tube. Central London, pretty much – with all the shops, people, sirens and pollution. I live in central London because it's where I grew up. I'm really not trying to be trendy living such an urban lifestyle. Like many people, I moved away for a couple of decades and then came home to roost to where my mum still lives, which happens to be half a mile up the road from King's Cross station.

When I was young, hot weekends were spent picking through the costume jewellery and vintage tea dresses at Camden Lock and wandering along the rubbish-strewn Regent's Canal looking for ways to get into London Zoo for free (you can't, trust me).

But my most memorable summers were in the country. When I was 13 my dad took me to the house of a friend in the Brecon Beacons, where I came across a waterfall with maidenhair ferns hanging off it and a wild white horse nibbling at a little lawn of grass as perfect as a bowling green. I thought it was some kind of magic. I associated these experiences with people, though – my father, my best friend's granny, who lived in Worcestershire and had an orchard and a hill you could roll down. I know it sounds silly, but I had no idea that these emotions were as much about the place as the people – these kind of realisations make you feel a fool, but the truth is when you're working, paying bills, bringing up children, caring for doddery parents, you don't really stop and think.

Now one of the greatest joys of this stage in my life is realising that I can access the countryside all by myself. I am stuck in Zone 2 for now, and I'm never going to afford a cottage with roses around the door – but I've bought a caravan by the sea, where you can drive for miles through the green tunnels of summer, enjoy a pint in a pub garden, stuff fish and chips on the beach.

I want my own children to share in the joy of taking a punt on the weather forecast (you know, the symbol with the black cloud but the rays of sunshine behind which has you saying, "Should we? Go on, let's do it. Take an anorak!") and then being rewarded with an unexpected clearing in the clouds. "I think it's brightening up!" must be one of the most overused expressions on a British staycation.

I want to give them pine-fringed sand dunes, grass snakes, dappled oak forests, hedgerows and ferns, dandelions and daisy chains. And after we stayed out all day, coming in and saying, "Well I think we had the best of it, didn't we?" Because we did.

Staycations – yes, they're officially a thing

✢ More than half of us (57%) now take their annual summer break in the UK – and the numbers are rising.
✢ The average staycation is one week.
✢ The nation's favourite countryside holiday destination is Cornwall, followed by Devon, the Cotswolds, the Lake District, the Scottish Highlands, North Wales and Bournemouth.
✢ The staycation industry is worth a huge £65 billion to the British economy.
✢ One in five holidays will include the family pet.

57% of us now take our annual summer break in the UK

LITERARY
Landscapes

Whether clambering up a craggy Yorkshire moor in search of Heathcliff, or taking a genteel stroll around Jane Austen's Bath, Britain's breathtaking locations are as diverse as the writers they inspired

LITERARY LANDSCAPES

Explore Haworth's cobbled streets, before a bracing walk on the moors

YORKSHIRE
THE BRONTES

The windswept moorlands of West Yorkshire brought endless inspiration to the Brontë sisters, Charlotte, Anne and Emily. They roamed the rugged landscape while conjuring up ideas for their novels, including Emily's *Wuthering Heights*, Charlotte's *Jane Eyre* and Anne's *The Tenant of Wildfell Hall*. The brooding South Pennines, aka Brontë Country, is studded with fascinating attractions. Visit the hilltop village of Haworth, with its original tea rooms and antiquated bookshops, and pop into the Brontë Parsonage Musuem – the Brontë family home from 1820 to 1861.

Now a world-famous museum, you can wander through the well-preserved living quarters and see original letters and manuscripts written by the famous siblings.

Numerous splendid walks from Haworth include the footpath to the Brontë Waterfalls – it's around 45 minutes from Haworth Main Street – and The Brontë Chair, a chair-shaped rock where the sisters are thought to have taken turns to sit and write their first stories. Part of the glorious 64km-long Brontë Way, this route leads through the valley and up to the moors, to Top Withens, a desolate ruin believed to be the setting for Heathcliff's farmstead in Wuthering Heights.

Where to stay The Dairy is a quirky semi-detached stone cottage with vintage fittings and a luxurious free-standing copper bath, just a few minutes from the centre of Haworth. To find out more visit sykescottages.co.uk >>

'A heaven so clear, an earth so calm'
Emily Brontë

WALES
DYLAN THOMAS

The true identity of Llareggub, the sleepy village in *Under Milk Wood*, has never been confirmed, but Laugharne, in the historic Welsh county of Carmarthenshire, has long staked a claim as Dylan Thomas's muse. Sitting on the estuary of the River Tâf, with its majestic Norman castle, this is where Wales' most celebrated poet spent the final years of his life. Take the two-mile Dylan Thomas Walk to see the views across the estuary and over the harbour to Thomas' writing shed, the Boathouse, where he lived from 1949 to 1953. Pause for a pint at one of the writer's favourite drinking spots, the Cross House Inn. Above the village is the graveyard of St Martin's Church, where the poet and his wife, Caitlin, are buried.
Where to stay The boutique Brown's Hotel in Laugharne was once Thomas' favourite drinking spot. To find out more head over to browns.wales

'We are not wholly bad or good, who live our lives under Milk Wood'
Under Milk Wood

BATH
JANE AUSTEN

When the author's father moved his family to Bath in the early 1800s, the city was a flourishing spa resort, much favoured by fashionable society. Jane Austen's time spent here inspired two of her famous novels, *Northanger Abbey* and *Persuasion*, and many of its Georgian features remain unchanged. Visit Bath Assembly Rooms, with its original crystal chandeliers – the setting for many balls depicted in *Northanger Abbey*. Also stop by at The Pump Room, frequented by the Austens. The Jane Austen Centre houses the Regency Tea Rooms, and a fascinating exhibition of costumes, manuscripts and film clips illustrate the city's influence on her work.
Where to stay Jane Austen's Residence at 4 Sydney Place, the author's former home, comprises 4 luxury apartments. To discover more, take a look at bathboutiquestays.co.uk

'Oh! Who can ever be tired of Bath?'
Northanger Abbey

LITERARY LANDSCAPES

SCOTLAND
JM BARRIE
The remote retreat of Eilean Shona was a source of endless inspiration for JM Barrie. 'It almost taketh the breath away to find so perfectly appointed a retreat on these wild shores,' he wrote in the 1920s, and it retains that power today. The private isle, in a tranquil loch near the isle of Skye, inspired the dream landscape of Neverland. Barrie spent a summer here, renting the island as a holiday home with his foster sons and their friends. They became the inspiration for the Darling family characters and the Lost Boys, plus the mischievous boy who never grew up — Barrie wrote the play script of *Peter Pan* here. Just a short boat ride from the mainland, the island is a haven of tranquillity — explore moss-covered woods, open hills and the sandy beach.
Where to stay Book one of the island's cottages, sleeps 2 or 4, or rent Eilean Shona House, sleeps 20, or the more intimate Shepherd's Cottage, sleeps 2; 01967 431 249, eileanshona.com

'Just think of happy things, and your heart will fly on wings, forever, in Never Never Land!' Peter Pan: Fairy Tales

DORSET
THOMAS HARDY
Explore the rolling landscape of Thomas Hardy's Wessex on a walking tour of Britain's first literature-themed long-distance path, the backdrop to many of the author's celebrated novels. Saunter between villages with thatched cottages and through chalky landscapes. Stop at the Inn in Cranborne where Hardy stayed, follow in Tess of the d'Urbervilles' footsteps to Win Green, and Shaftesbury (Shaston in *Jude the Obscure*).
Where to stay A walking holiday created with Margaret Marande, author of *The Hardy Way – A 19th-century Pilgrimage*, takes in the highlights. For more, head to inntravel.co.uk

Or book in to Chesil Cottage, with sea views over the stunning Chesil Beach — Hardy's house, Max Gate, and Hardy's Cottage are a few miles away. Sleeps 4, nationaltrust.org.uk/holidays/chesil-cottage-dorset >>

'God was palpably present in the country, and the devil had gone with the world to town' Far from the Madding Crowd

ENGLISH RIVIERA
AGATHA CHRISTIE

Dame Agatha Christie loved Devon, and it's rich with landmarks that'll fascinate fans of the Queen of Crime. Walk the Agatha Christie Mile along the seafront at Torquay, her birthplace, to see various spots that were intrinsic to the author's life, including the secluded bay where she liked to swim. Take a trip to the eerie caves at Kents Cavern, a short distance from Torquay's town centre, to view where she found inspiration for Hampsley Cavern in *The Man in the Brown Suit*. Six miles down the coast you'll find Greenway House, the Christie family's beloved holiday home, carefully preserved by the National Trust. And any Christie fanatic should pay a visit to Burgh Island, the author's writing retreat, with its sandy beaches and silver seas. This wonderful little tidal island is well known as the setting for *And Then There Were None* and *Evil Under the Sun*.

Where to stay The iconic Burgh Island Hotel, fully restored to its 1930s glamour, offers rooms including Agatha's Beach House. Find out more details on their website at burghisland.com

'Devon is so beautiful, those hills and the red cliffs...' And Then There Were None

FOREST OF DEAN
JRR TOLKIEN

The Royal Forest of Dean in Gloucestershire is where you'll be surrounded by the magic of Tolkien's Middle-earth. The author is believed to have been a frequent visitor here, influenced by its rich folklore – a walk through the tangled primordial forest's Puzzlewood conjures up the intricate landscapes of his *The Lord of the Rings* trilogy and *The Hobbit*. With mossy rocks, twisted roots, woodland bridges, and pathways winding through the gullies, you'll almost expect to spot a hobbit or two. The surrounding ancient Forest of Dean also offers forested hillsides, with ancient villages, castles, museums and cathedrals to discover.

Where to stay Check into Lower Wythall B&B, Herefordshire, 10 minutes from Puzzlewood. Set in a Grade II Elizabethan timber-framed house, with 1.3 acres of gardens, it enjoys views across the Wye Valley Area of Outstanding Natural Beauty. Find out more by visiting lowerwythall.co.uk

'The wide world is all about you: you can fence yourselves in, but you cannot forever fence it out'
JRR Tolkien

LITERARY LANDSCAPES

CUMBRIA
WILLIAM WORDSWORTH

The Romantic poet William Wordsworth's beloved Lake District celebrated the 250th anniversary of his birth throughout 2020, and planned lots of new things to see and do, thanks to the Wordsworth Trust's multimillion-pound Reimagining Wordsworth project. Dove Cottage, the poet's former home, sees new exhibits including sister Dorothy Wordsworth's *The Grasmere Journals*, and a recreation of the family's beloved orchard. The Wordsworth Museum is also being expanded and modernised, providing views of the surrounding fells, giving you the chance to stop and reflect on the landscape that brought to life many of the poet's finest masterpieces. Wander lonely as a cloud around Ullswater, the inspiration for Wordsworth's most famous lyric poem, *Daffodils*, and check in at his birthplace at Cockermouth, presented exactly as it would have been in the 1770s, with a garden full of fruits, vegetables and flowers, and an open fire burning in the kitchen.
Where to stay Grasmere, in the heart of this newly designated World Heritage Site, was described by Wordsworth as 'the loveliest spot that man hath ever found'. Stay in the heart of the village at Herdwick Cottage, a traditional slate hideaway. Find out more at the website sallyscottages.co.uk/herdwick-cottage

'The loveliest spot that man hath ever found'
William Wordsworth

Six of the best... UK WALKING HOTSPOTS

From views atop a Wainwright in the Lakes to the power of the Cornish coast, there's nowhere like the UK for a fantastic place to walk

BEST FOR BREATH-TAKING VIEWS

BEST FOR A TOTAL ESCAPE

THE LAKE DISTRICT

Put on the map (literally) by walker Alfred Wainwright, under whose name 214 peaks are logged, the Lake District is a dramatic and beautiful place. Towering above the lakes are hills and mountains such as Scafell Pike and Skiddaw. Stay in one of the surrounding towns — Keswick, Windermere or Grasmere. They've all got pubs for a post-walk drink, such as the Royal Oak in Keswick (royaloakkeswick.co.uk) or rent a cottage from Sally's Cottages (sallyscottages.co.uk).

✳ **FIND OUT MORE** Visit the website at lakedistrict.gov.uk

THE SCOTTISH HIGHLANDS AND THE WEST HIGHLAND WAY

Head up on the sleeper train to Edinburgh and then beyond to the highlands, where vast valleys and heather-covered hillsides hide stag as you trek. To add a dose of history, make Glencoe your base, scene of the massacre in 1692. Opt for self-catering — like Bluebell Cottage (bluebellcottageglencoe.co.uk) — or for luxury, try Glencoe House (glencoe-house.com) and Schloss Hotel in Roxburge (schlosshotel-roxburghe.com).

✳ **FIND OUT MORE** Visit the website at walkhighlands.co.uk

UK WALKING HOTSPOTS

BEST FOR A RUGGED COASTAL BREAK

BEST FOR MINGLING WITH THE A-LIST

THE SOUTH WEST COAST PATH
This path covers some of the most rugged coastline in the UK, where you can spot seals in the Atlantic waters – and visit some of the locations for the BBC series *Poldark*. If you have time, it takes 52 days to walk the entire path. Alternatively, walk a section in a weekend or on a week's break and for extra inspiration, take a copy of *The Salt Path* by Raynor Winn. It charts the author's journey from sudden homelessness to walking the path with a tent. Farm Stay has cosy cottages to choose from (farmstay.co.uk) but if you're looking for luxury, try Salcombe Harbour Hotel & Spa (harbourhotels.co.uk/salcombe).
* **FIND OUT MORE** Visit the website at southwestcoastpath.org.uk

THE COTSWOLDS
One of the most picturesque and upmarket country retreats, the Cotswolds is packed with pretty stone houses, antiques shops and cosy pubs – not to mention the likes of Kate Moss, David Cameron and other household names with homes here. Stay in one of the towns to explore this designated Area of Outstanding Natural Beauty, such as Chipping Campden, Bourton-on-the-Water or Burford, which also has a lovely tea room and cheese shop. The Fox pub in Chipping Norton (foxchippingnorton.co.uk) has rooms, or for decadence, head to boutique hotel Thyme (thyme.co.uk/accommodation).
* **FIND OUT MORE** Visit the website at cotswoldsaonb.org.uk

BEST FOR ANIMAL LOVERS

BEST FOR COUNTRY CHARM

THE NEW FOREST
They're synonymous with this part of the country and you won't be able to go far without seeing a New Forest pony while out walking, as they roam free. This area's great for people who prefer a flatter walk. Keep with the 'at one with nature' vibe by staying in a log cabin complete with swimming pool (newforestdot.com) or go for glamour at The Pig – a group of boutique hotels focusing on local food with an outpost in Brockenhurst (thepighotel.com).
* **FIND OUT MORE** Visit the website at thenewforest.co.uk

THE NORTH YORK MOORS NATIONAL PARK
Yorkshire might be best-known for its Dales, but closer to the east coast lies the equally impressive North York Moors National Park. Combine a stay on the coast in historic Whitby with some yomps across the moorland heather. Lovely walks include hill Roseberry Topping – base yourself in Helmsley, staying in the Feversham Arms hotel and spa (fevershamarmshotel.com) or the dog-friendly Black Swan (blackswan-helmsley.co.uk). In spring, visit Farndale for a feast of daffodils.
* **FIND OUT MORE** Visit the website at northyorkmoors.org.uk

MINDFUL TRAVEL | 65

Taking the WATERS

From glorious lakes and rivers to thundering waterfalls, enjoy some of the UK's most beautiful and inspiring wild waters

A beautiful underwater arch, fed by a waterfall, can be seen in one of the Fairy Pools if you go for a swim.

TAKING THE WATERS

FAIRY POOLS, ISLE OF SKYE

It's easy to imagine fairies dancing in the vibrant turquoise pools that lie in the foothills of the jagged Black Cuillin Mountains. As the River Brittle shimmies to the sea, it creates waterfalls, streamlets, stepping stones and pools of crystal water surrounded by ferns, purple heather and lichen. On a sunny day, the pools' greens and blues are at their best, lit up to create a magical realm. Look out for rabbits and deer, as well as meadow pipits and curlews, plus orchids, sundews and carnivorous blue and purple butterwort.
WONDERFUL WALK The 5km circular walk from the Fairy Pools car park to the furthest waterfall is dotted with burbling waterfalls. You can continue further up away from the crowds along the trail all the way to the base of the mountain.
✱ **FIND OUT MORE** Visit the website at walkhighlands.co.uk

LLYN IDWAL, SNOWDONIA

Snowdonia's stunning mountain range hides some marvellous 'secret' lakes, including Llyn Idwal, enveloped by a bowl of rock dating back 450 million years. This small glacial lake has its own pebble beach where you can brave the icy waters for a dip. Cushions of ancient purple saxifrage grow among the craggy basalt rocks, as do lemony yellow alpine rose root and sprays of water lobelia.
WONDERFUL WALK Take a dramatic valley hike through Cwm Idwal from the Snowdonia National Park Visitor Centre to the llyn (lake), passing wild goats as well as the rocks where Sir Edmund Hillary trained for Everest. Walk around the lake, or schlep up to Devil's Kitchen, a crag that often ejects plumes of steam.
✱ **FIND OUT MORE** Visit the website at nationaltrust.org.uk >>

Cwm Idwal was a favourite haunt of Sir Charles Darwin during his studies and investigations into evolution.

MINDFUL TRAVEL | 67

This hilltop spot is run by a group of local volunteers who rescued it from closure in 2001.

GADDINGS DAM, YORKSHIRE

Brooding Gaddings Dam at Todmorden, in the South Pennines, sits 355m above sea level. The land here is rated a Site of Special Scientific Interest, with protected birdlife, plants and wild flowers. Popular among wild swimmers, its sandy shore was formed by weathering of the sandstone used to build the reservoir, creating what is known as Britain's highest beach. It's a lovely spot to enjoy the lapping water, or follow the trail around the water's edge.
WONDERFUL WALK Take the 7km loop from Walsden village, pausing at the Basin Stone, a weathered outcrop of millstone grit, on the way. The path gets very steep, and the dam remains hidden until you reach it, but there are magnificent views over Todmorden at the top.
✱ **FIND OUT MORE** Visit the website at gaddingsdam.org

NORFOLK BROADS

The fabulous Norfolk Broads are a unique hodgepodge of feathery reed beds, meandering waterways, tangled woodlands and wide-open reaches with enormous skies. The area is a haven for wildlife – a quarter of Britain's rare and endangered species live here, including water voles, cuckoos and European eels. Look out for water-loving plants such as frothy meadowsweet and milk parsley, which are a refuge for swallowtail butterflies.
WONDERFUL WALK Amble from How Hill to Ludham Bridge, along the banks of the River Ant and Buttle Marsh nature reserve, home to otters and swifts. It's 4km to Ludham Bridge, a hamlet with a riverside cafe.
✱ **FIND OUT MORE** Visit the website at broads.co.uk

Quirky colloquial names for the Broads' wonders include 'umpty-tump' (molehill) and 'bishy-barney-bee' (ladybird).

KENNET AND AVON CANAL, WILTSHIRE

Passing through spectacular landscapes, the Kennet and Avon Canal is a 140km-long sparkly necklace studded with pretty towns and villages. Created at the turn of the 19th century to link London's waterways with the Bristol Channel, it provides a vibrant wildlife corridor – look out for herons and kingfishers, as well as grey wagtails and marsh tits. Water lilies bloom on the water, while purple loosestrife attracts brimstone butterflies and elephant hawk moths.
WONDERFUL WALK Stroll along the Caen Hill Locks to the Avon valley.
✱ **FIND OUT MORE** Visit the website at canalrivertrust.org.uk

Wildlife of the Kennet and Avon Canal by Mark C Baker includes wildlife-spotting hints and tips, as well as colour photos.

TAKING THE WATERS

ULLSWATER, LAKE DISTRICT

Wordsworth described the curving lake at Ullswater as 'the happiest combination of beauty and grandeur which any of the lakes affords'. Staggeringly scenic, tranquil and unspoilt, the lake meanders in and out of the surrounding hills and towering peaks, while wild flowers dot the landscape – look out for wild thyme, harebells and grass of parnassus.
WONDERFUL WALK The Ullswater Way is a glorious 30km trail that circumnavigates the whole lake. Take the 10km stretch from Pooley Bridge to see Aira Force, which is a thundering waterfall of sensational natural beauty.
✷ FIND OUT MORE Visit the website at ullswater.co.uk

> Peer into Ullswater's crystal-clear water and you might spot brown trout or rare Ice Age relics, Arctic char.

WHITELADY WATERFALL, LYDFORD GORGE, DEVON

The spectacular chasm at Lydford, the deepest river gorge in the South West, holds the beautiful 30m-high Whitelady waterfall. Here, wind and spray from the impact of water on rocks provide a rainforest-like environment that nurtures a host of plant life, including mosses and ferns. Ravens and buzzards circle the sky, while kingfishers and otters dip in and out of the waters.
WONDERFUL WALK From the National Trust car park, explore the steep winding paths to the waterfall, stopping by to admire the of roaring whirlpools known as the 'Devil's Cauldron', so called because the water appears to be boiling. Tunnel Falls, a series of potholes formed by river erosion, are another highlight.
✷ FIND OUT MORE Visit the website at nationaltrust.org.uk

> Local legend says the Whitelady Waterfall is named after a ghostly woman, who's been spotted wandering the landscape.

LOUGH NEAGH, NORTHERN IRELAND

Dubbed 'Ulster's inland sea', gleaming Lough Neagh is the largest freshwater lake in the British isles. The lush countryside and nature reserves that surround it make it a joy to explore; a number of rare fen plant species can be found here, while the wetland meadows are rich in wild flower species including sneezewort, fleabane and ragged robin.
WONDERFUL WALK The 7km trail of the Oxford Island Nature Reserve has a range of habitats, and don't miss Kinnego Marina.
✷ FIND OUT MORE Visit the website at walkni.com

MINDFUL TRAVEL | 69

Six of the best...
UK SWIM SPOTS

Whether you're practising your front crawl in a river, lapping it up lakeside or sea bathing, reap the benefits of taking a dip outdoors

BEST FOR A BREAK FROM THE CITY

BEST FOR WEEKEND ADVENTURE

THE SERPENTINE LIDO, HYDE PARK, LONDON

Over 150 years old, the Serpentine Swimming Club (who meet here every day between 5-9.30am) is the oldest in Britain. Having hosted the swimming section of the Olympic triathlon in 2012, the lido is popular with triathletes too. But you don't need to be a pro to experience this watery nirvana. Reassuringly, the plethora of plant life means the water is clean and clear, so you can enjoy wild swimming right in the heart of central London.

RIVER THAMES, PANGBOURNE, BERKSHIRE

The River Thames might conjure up images of murky, polluted waters snaking through the capital that you wouldn't even think of dipping your toe into, let alone your head. But the famous waterway has more picturesque settings earlier along its route before it reaches the Big Smoke. Located on the edge of the Chiltern Hills, within easy reach of London, this section is unspoilt and a LOT cleaner. Parts of the river are wooded for a more secluded dip, and the surrounding meadows offer an ideal opportunity for a post-plunge picnic.

UK SWIM SPOTS

BEST FOR PURE ESCAPISM

BEST FOR THE WILD SWIMMING NEWBIE

BUDE SEA POOL, BUDE, CORNWALL

Want a salty hit and protection from the unpredictable current? This spot is for you. This beautiful, part natural, part man-made tidal swimming pool is set into the rocks at Summerleaze Beach. Constructed in 1930, it has provided safe bathing in Bude for almost 90 years. The pool, which measures around 91m long and 45m wide, is topped up by the sea at high tide each day. But be careful when entering – as it's part natural, it's hard to give an exact depth, particularly as the environment changes with the tide.

LOCH MORLICH, NEAR AVIEMORE, SCOTLAND

Scotland's open access laws (meaning you can swim pretty much anywhere) make the thousands of freshwater lochs in Scotland a haven for wild swimmers. In the heart of the Cairngorms, this loch is surrounded by stunning views. You might have to dodge a few windsurfers and kayakers, but popularity brings great amenities – you can hire wetsuits (yes, the water is a little fresh!), and warm up afterwards at the shoreline café. It also boasts Scotland's only award-winning freshwater beach, so you can catch some rays between dips too.

Swimming can burn over 300 calories in just 30 minutes!

BEST FOR THE ADRENALINE JUNKIE

BEST FOR STUNNING VIEWS

KAILPOT CRAG, ULLSWATER, LAKE DISTRICT

Like the "wild" side of open water swimming? Then dive right in. This high, craggy cliff beneath Hallin Fell plummets into deep water, making this lake ideal for jumping and snorkelling. Or for those looking for a more serene swim, you can access the water via the shingle beaches that pepper the shoreline. Thanks to glaciation (the process of being covered by glaciers or ice sheets), Ullswater has excellent water quality, and as it faces west, it means you can enjoy the sunset.

RHOSSILI BAY, GOWER PENINSULA, SOUTH WALES

Voted the best beach in Wales and third in the UK in the TripAdvisor Travellers' Choice Awards, this is a must-swim. This impressive stretch of Celtic coastline offers three miles of breathtaking views, which takes in one of Gower's most famous landmarks, Worms Head. Shaped like a giant sea serpent, it marks the most westerly tip of Gower. It's also a wildlife haven, with a variety of cliff-nesting birds. Tides can be vicious though, so if the sea looks churned up, don't swim.

MINDFUL TRAVEL | 71

It's a SHORE THING

UK travel may have been curtailed by the current crisis – but it means we appreciate our beautiful island more than ever. Here's our celebration of some jaw-dropping coastlines

The 'tilt' of the rocks exposes 185 million years of history, from the Triassic, Jurassic and Cretaceous periods.

Whether you yearn to clamber up soaring cliffsides, trundle through tidal marshes or gaze at prehistoric limestone arches, Britain's glorious coastline has plenty for everyone, from blustery coastal walks to windswept Atlantic strands, as well as the traditional seaside.

JURASSIC COAST, DORSET

The Jurassic Coast is up there with the Great Barrier Reef as one of the world's natural wonders. Stretching from Exmouth in east Devon to Studland Bay, Dorset, it's one of Earth's richest sites for prehistoric remains and fossils, with an unparalleled range of dramatic natural features.

WHERE TO WALK Stroll from Lulworth Cove, where you can explore the folded limestone rocks of Stair Hole, then over the cliffs to see Durdle Door. From here stroll the sands of Man O'War beach, or head higher over the crags of Bats Head.
✴ **FIND OUT MORE** Visit the website at walkingbritain.co.uk

IT'S A SHORE THING

ATLANTIC COAST, CORNWALL

Cornwall's Atlantic coast, a thrilling landscape carved and sculpted by the pounding sea and surf, is made all the more exciting by the numerous tales of smuggling and wrecking that abound in her coves and caves.

WHERE TO WALK The bracing 5km clifftop walk from St Agnes to Perranporth walk brings splendid vistas. Starting at the Driftwood Spars, walk up the path to the clifftops for amazing views of Trevaunance Cove. This walk trails over turquoise coves only accessible by kayak, through ancient quarries and over disused mines. As you round into Perranporth, watch the relentless waves coming in against the backdrop of Perranporth's dramatic standalone cliffs with their craggy, weather-beaten holes.

✱ **FIND OUT MORE** Visit the website at southwestcoastpath.org.uk

At 192m high, St Agnes Beacon was used during the Napoleonic Wars, when it would be lit at sightings of French ships.

SUTHERLAND, SCOTTISH HIGHLANDS

Covering miles of dazzling scenic coastline along the northernmost tip of Britain, remote Sutherland is the hidden gem of the Scottish Highlands, with rugged cliffs, perfect coves of white sand, incredible azure blue waters and dunes of sea-green marram grass. If you're after wide open spaces, wilderness and complete isolation, this is the place to be.

WHERE TO WALK Take the 6km path via Alltan'abradhan to Achmelvich beach, where you'll find clear turquoise water and pristine sand juxtaposed with jagged rocks and rugged hills. Start in the Achmelvich beach car park and follow the footpath over the grassy coastal hills, stopping at the old grain mill on your way. Extend your walk further to discover Hermit's Castle: at just 10sq m, it's the smallest in Europe.

✱ **FIND OUT MORE** Visit the website at walkhighlands.co.uk >>

Sutherland has the highest cliffs on mainland Great Britain, at Clo Mor near Durness. They rise to nearly 300m.

SEVEN SISTERS, SUSSEX

A magnificent series of white chalk cliffs line the coast edging the Sussex South Downs, plunging dramatically into the cerulean sea and comprising one of England's most striking coastal spectacles. They're considered both whiter and more scenic than their cousins in Dover. The Seven Sisters stretch from Cuckmere Haven to Birling Gap in East Sussex, where kittiwakes and fulmars can be seen alongside Brimstone butterflies and flowering cowslips in spring and summer.

WHERE TO WALK Start the Seven Sisters walk at Birling Gap, taking the South Downs Way along the clifftops. At low tide, you may be able to see the wreck of Coonatto, a Barquentine clipper. At Haven Brow you can head inland from Cuckmere Haven, rumoured to be a former smugglers' landing site.

✱ **FIND OUT MORE** Visit the website at nationaltrust.org.uk

> You can still see WW2 'dragon's teeth' pillboxes and anti-tank defences scattered across the cliffs at Seven Sisters.

NORTHUMBERLAND

> This coast is one of the most significant areas in Europe for the Atlantic grey seal, found all year round.

With dramatic arcs of windswept sands, craggy cliffs and brooding castles overlooking the icy North Sea, it's easy to see why much of Northumberland's coastline has been designated an Area of Outstanding Natural Beauty. It's a walker's delight; there are around 40 miles of dramatic 'Heritage' shores to marvel at, and with a coastal path running from Berwick-upon-Tweed all the way to the River Coquet, it's perfect for walkers and nature lovers.

WHERE TO WALK Take the 10km amble from Craster to Low Newton, via Dunstanburgh Castle.

✱ **FIND OUT MORE** Visit the website at nationaltrust.org.uk

NORTH NORFOLK

Wild, peaceful and expansive, North Norfolk's beautiful coast stretches between the resort of Hunstanton and the pretty town of Sheringham, a spectacular landscape of tidal marshes, creeks, shingle spits, and sweeping golden beaches backed by pine woods. Further east is the imperious clifftop setting of Cromer, with its Victorian pier striding proudly out to sea. The coastline then meanders southward to secluded villages such as Mundesley and Happisburgh, with its striped lighthouse.

WHERE TO WALK The 8km stroll from Wells to Holkham is a joy. Starting at Wells beach car park, walk past the iconic beach huts until you reach the vast, tree-framed sands at Holkham. Return along the Norfolk Coast Path through the cool pine forest.

✱ **FIND OUT MORE** Visit the website at gps-routes.co.uk

IT'S A SHORE THING

CAUSEWAY COAST, NORTHERN IRELAND

Overlooking the crashing North Atlantic Ocean, the spectacular Causeway Coast is a land of myth and legend as well as stunning views, with toe-tingling cliffs, beaches, forests, headlands, rocks and ancient landforms. During summer, wild flowers bring this unique landscape to life; look out for blue spring squill, pink thrift and white sea campion bursting into flower. The Causeway Coastal Route encompasses some remarkable landmarks, including the nail-biting Carrick-a-Rede Rope Bridge just outside Ballintoy, the ruins of Downhill Demesne and the world-famous Giant's Causeway.

WHERE TO WALK The jaunt from Portstewart to Ballycastle, a 16km slice of the Causeway Coast walking route, boasts some of the most spectacular scenery in the area. The path hugs the shore all the way to Giant's Causeway.

✱ **FIND OUT MORE** Visit the website at walkni.com

Many of the famous scenes from the TV drama Game of Thrones were filmed along the Causeway Coast.

Cromer Shoals Chalk Bed is the longest in the world, and is home to sea slugs, harbour porpoises and seals.

PEMBROKESHIRE, WALES

Pembrokeshire's coastline is an intricate ribbon of weather-beaten, flower-dotted cliffs, dazzling beaches and tiny secret coves, bejewelled with rock pools. From St Dogmaels in the north to Amroth in the south, the landscape covers steep limestone cliffs, undulating red sandstone bays, volcanic headlands, estuaries and flooded glacial valleys.

WHERE TO WALK A wonderful 6km circular route around St David's peninsula starts at Whitesands and circumnavigates Pembrokeshire's rugged coastal headland. Visit the 4,000-year-old Neolithic burial chamber en route, and take in the views over Whitesands Bay and out to sea towards Ramsey Island.

✱ **FIND OUT MORE** Visit the website at nationaltrust.org.uk

Twittering flocks of linnets are one of the glorious sounds of summer on the Pembrokeshire coastline.

MINDFUL TRAVEL | 75

Treasure ISLANDS

From wonderful windswept wildernesses to bucket-and-spade holiday favourites, the UK has more than 1,000 beautiful islands dotted around its rivers and coastline. Here are just a few precious British offshore delights just waiting to be discovered

TREASURE ISLANDS

MERSEA, ESSEX

Across a narrow channel from Essex's southern coast, Mersea offers a seaswept dose of nature and traditional beach life. Here you'll find Jurassic cliffs, sandy beaches, bleakly beautiful mudflats, pretty pastel beach huts, and even a vineyard. You can walk around the whole island, a popular 20km challenge, to admire the views and wildlife — look out for marsh harriers, water voles, red squirrels and numerous migrating seabirds. Mersea oysters make their way into the kitchens of everyone from Gordon Ramsay to The Ritz — but they taste their best eaten right here, in one of the oyster bars or beach shacks. Mersea is cut off from the mainland when the high tide rises above the Strood, the causeway that joins the island to the mainland. >>

Rare and protected species of flora found around Mersea include yellow horned poppy, prickly sea holly and sea campion.

TIREE, INNER HEBRIDES

The most westerly island of the Inner Hebrides and the 'Hawaii of the north', Tiree is a windswept, treeless 'desert island' with fewer than 700 inhabitants. Graced with prime fertile land and sparkling white beaches, it has an abundance of sunshine in the warm seasons, and the blustery elements attract countless wind surfers. Walkers will enjoy nearly 60km of mainly flat coastline, complete with a plethora of craggy inlets and glorious deserted beaches. Ferries to Tiree depart from Oban, or fly from Glasgow.

Tiree has an ancient 'ringing stone', a large boulder that balances on other rocks and emits a metallic ring when struck gently.

FAIR ISLE, SHETLAND

Fair Isle, the most remote inhabited island in the UK, is home to just 55 residents, all happily engaged in crofting and arts and crafts amid a menagerie of sheep, goats, cows, pigs, ducks and various seabirds. Famous for its knitwear and historic shipwrecks, this tiny gem, halfway between Orkney and mainland Shetland, has lots of fabulous walks – try the 'Complete Fair Isle', a 15km trek that takes in the island's famous bird sanctuary. Catch a flight or overnight ferry to Shetland from Aberdeen, then a flight or ferry to Fair Isle.

During the summer months, Shetland is bathed in near-perpetual daylight, with a silver sheen at midnight – the 'simmer dim'.

TREASURE ISLANDS

ISLE OF MAN

Mountainous and cliff-fringed, the Isle of Man's patchwork of delights includes golden beaches, snow-capped peaks, wooded glens, rural villages and steam trains straight out of a 1950s picture book. This self-governing island, nestled between Ireland and England, offers rollicking rambles along windswept coastlines and rugged hills – try climbing to the summit of 620m-high Snaefell mountain, the island's highest peak, accessible via the mountain railway. Take a boat trip to the Calf of Man, a tiny islet, to see spectacular seabird colonies. Ferries to the capital Douglas depart from Liverpool, Birkenhead, Heysham or Belfast.

The Isle of Man is the only location where you can see England, Scotland, Wales and Northern Ireland at once, from the top of Snaefell.

LUNDY, DEVON

Adrift in protected coral waters in the Bristol Channel, Lundy is a blissful reef of granite and heathland. They don't call it 'Britain's Galapagos' for nothing – its wildlife includes puffins, rabbits, seals, guillemots, deer, feral goats and basking sharks. As England's first marine wildlife reserve, it boasts great diving sites, with shipwrecks and sea creatures to marvel at. Take the 12km circular walk and you'll stumble across burial chambers, former prison caves and the highest lighthouse in Britain, as well as some fascinating flora and fauna, including the incredibly rare Lundy Cabbage plant. Ferries depart from Bideford or Ilfracombe.

Buy a map from the island's only shop and try the 'letterbox' treasure hunt, which takes you to 27 of the island's secret gems.

GUERNSEY, CHANNEL ISLANDS

Charming Guernsey oozes contentedness – even its famous cows appear to be in a state of bliss. Part of the island's appeal is its jumble of influences – it feels a little bit French and quite a lot British, and the relics from the German occupation during World War Two add interest. Take a stroll around St Peter Port, where Victor Hugo wrote *Les Misérables* or clamber up to the 800-year-old Castle Cornet, to admire the landscapes that inspired some of Renoir's loveliest paintings. >>

YNYS LLANDDWYN, WALES

Ynys Llanddwyn is a small tidal island off the west coast of Anglesey, in north-west Wales. This rocky paradise boasts a 'holy' freshwater well, the ruins of a 16th-century church dedicated to St Dwynwen (the Welsh patron saint of lovers), an ancient lighthouse and some of the oldest volcanic rocks in Wales. There are gorgeous beaches and you can snorkel for crab and lobster among the kelp beds. The island is 1km south of the village of Newborough — check the tide times before you cross to the island.

The Tŵr Mawr lighthouse, on the tip of Ynys Llanddwyn, marks the western entrance to the Menai Strait.

ISLE OF WIGHT

The Isle of Wight off the south coast of England mixes beautiful landscapes with old-fashioned English charm. There are red squirrels in the forests, and Mediterranean plants flourish among the plunging hills of Ventnor and the Undercliff. Nearly half the island is designated an Area of Outstanding Natural Beauty, and the 800km of well-maintained footpaths that criss-cross the island make it a walker's dream. Stroll the 5km stretch from Brook to Freshwater, taking in the stunning views along the sandstone cliffs to Compton Bay to find fossil remains and dinosaur footprints at low tide. Ferries depart from Portsmouth and Lymington.

Autumn is the best time to see rare wildfowl, such as wigeons, grey plovers and bar-tailed godwits, which overwinter on Lindisfarne.

LINDISFARNE/HOLY ISLAND, NORTHUMBERLAND

Isolated by fast-moving tides that submerge the causeway twice a day, the brooding Holy Island of Lindisfarne is shrouded in history and mythology. The isle is dominated by its 16th-century castle, which rises from sheer rock at the tip of the island. You'll find some marvellous scenery, from beautiful deserted beaches to majestic dunes teeming with wildlife. The dune-covered area in the north is part of the Lindisfarne National Nature Reserve and has many rare species, including pretty sea aster and grass of parnassus. Grey seals bob in the waters and sun themselves on the sands, and there are roe deer and glorious sunsets.

TREASURE ISLANDS

TRESCO, ISLES OF SCILLY, CORNWALL

Gloriously isolated and unspoilt, the Isles of Scilly form an archipelago of more than 200 stunning subtropical islands, islets and rocks, 50km off the tip of Cornwall. White sand beaches, tranquil coves and wild flower meadows provide a sanctuary for wildlife and migrating birds. Verdant Tresco packs a lot in-between its shores. The rugged north, with its historic forts and spectacular views, is a treat for walkers and explorers, while in the west, the beautiful Abbey Gardens thread through exquisite walled enclosures and terraces, displaying 20,000 exotic plants. You can fly to the Isles of Scilly from Land's End, Newquay or Exeter, or for a more leisurely sea journey take the ferry from Penzance.

Don't miss Tresco's Valhalla collection of 30 ships' figureheads, rescued from shipwrecked vessels over the centuries.

RATHLIN, NORTHERN IRELAND

Around 100 people live alongside a spectacular array of wildlife on Rathlin, Northern Ireland's only inhabited island. Sitting just north of Ballycastle on the rugged North Antrim Coast, the L-shaped isle is steeped in cultural heritage and awash with seafaring history – a number of shipwrecks here include a World War One cruiser, now a national monument. Take the hike from Rathlin Harbour to the RSPB Roonivoolin Reserve to enjoy views of seals, Irish hare and curlew. Ferries to Rathlin leave from Ballycastle.

Visit Rathlin's quirky upside-down lighthouse, built into a cliff face, which is now home to the RSPB's Rathlin West Light Seabird Centre.

WONDERFUL WORLD

84 *Recharge in Palm Springs*
Life is one big pool party in this desert oasis – and so much more…

88 *Feel well in West Hollywood*
This small city in Los Angeles has a lot to offer the health-conscious traveller

90 *A natural wonder*
Yosemite National Park is one of the world's most iconic sights

92 *Magical Mexico*
Whale-watching, tequila-tasting and golden sands in Puerto Vallarta

96 *Paradise islands*
It's an irresistible destination if you love clear seas, blue skies and white sands

102 *Wild wellness in Mauritius*
Yoga, meditation and a mindful walk through a tropical rainforest…

104 *Breathtaking Cambodia*
A trip to Vietnam's Mekong Delta and Cambodia's luxury island retreats

108 *Off the beaten track*
Ho Tram Beach is an oasis of calm on the coast of Vietnam

110 *Million pound mountains*
Dubai isn't just glitzy high-rises and boozy brunches

112 *Living la dolce vita*
We've sampled some of Italy's finest and best treasures

118 *Learn to live the bella figura*
How self-care the Italian way can make you happier and healthier

120 *Recipe for success*
For Santa Montefiore, learning the art of Italian home cooking was perfect

122 *Three go mad in Ibiza*
Reinventing the girls' holiday once the children have left home

124 *Mountain mayhem!*
An Austrian activity holiday for mind, body and soul

112

122

84

104

92

MINDFUL TRAVEL

Recharge in PALM SPRINGS

Life is one big pool party in this desert oasis – but it also has an impressive Hollywood legacy, hiking trails and breathtaking landscapes, which should elevate Palm Springs straight to the top of your travel wish-list

"The city is surrounded by palm trees and framed by the dramatic backdrop of the San Jacinto Mountains"

RECHARGE IN PALM SPRINGS

Anyone who's new to Palm Springs soon asks the question: how do they keep their landscapes so vividly green? The city may be sat in a dusty plain of ground-hugging cacti, with sunshine 350 days of the year, but the town is miraculously sustained by huge, deep aquifers.

These supply the million sprinklers that keep Palm Springs' lawns and golf courses luminously lush, and the high bougainvillea hedges refreshed. Even diners at street cafes are regularly spritzed by a fine, cooling mist while they eat. Which, when summer temperatures reach 40 degrees, you'll be endlessly grateful for.

It's easy to overlook the boulevards of Palm Springs when planning a trip to the US, especially if your sights are set on the spangly tourist attractions of Los Angeles, but this city in southern California is the ultimate feel-good, laid-back destination. Whether flying in to Palm Springs International Airport or driving from Los Angeles (a good run will take two hours), as soon as you reach the iconic wind turbines — which provide power for the entire valley — you can feel your mood lighten. There's something about the dry desert heat that will make even the itchiest feet feel utterly relaxed. No wonder Californians come here in their droves whenever they can.

Unwinding poolside

Our hotel, ARRIVE, is just over a mile from the heart of downtown Palm Springs, so you have easy access to the city's lively shopping, food and festival scene.

Yet with just 32 rooms, its laid-back feel is refreshingly peaceful. When you check in at the bar (there's no lobby), you'll even get a free cocktail to get you in the mood to relax.

Palm Springs is the land of swimming pools, in every shape and size. The day begins and ends in the water. The truth is, we could have spent the entire break lounging by the hotel pool, surrounded by palm trees and framed by the dramatic backdrop of the San Jacinto Mountains. But we were keen to explore Palm Springs itself.

Party with the rat pack

We drove around town in an open-top Mustang, channelling Frank Sinatra and all the other Rat Packers whose spirit still lingers. In the 1950s and 60s, Palm Springs was the ultimate swinging getaway for Sinatra, Elvis and a whole host of Hollywood stars.

During this time, Hollywood actors were contracted to be no more than two hours' drive away from the film studios, and Palm Springs just happened to be the furthest they could go. Over the decades, far from the media's prying eyes, the likes of Clark Gable, Marilyn Monroe and Frank Sinatra created a hedonistic playground, built by a roll-call of leading architects — Richard Neutra, Donald Wexler, John Lautner — whose distinctive style is now labelled mid-century modern.

Back in 1946, when Frank Sinatra had made his first million, he celebrated by commissioning a new house in the city where he hosted >>

The ARRIVE hotel reflects the city's famous mid-century modern style

MINDFUL TRAVEL | 85

the most glamorous parties of the day. With motor-driven glass sliding doors, state-of-the-art recording equipment, a piano-shaped pool and a flagpole (used to let friends know it was cocktail hour), it was the epitome of cool. If you want to party like Sinatra, you can now rent his former home for £2,000 a night.

A multitude of modern celebs have set up residence, from Leonardo DiCaprio and Brad Pitt, to former President Obama and family. Drop by the Visitors Centre – worth seeing even to take a glance at the space-age structure, which was originally built in 1965 as a petrol station – and purchase a $5 map of Modern Palm Springs for a self-guided tour of celebrity homes, past and present.

Desert modernism

If you want to go a step further and have a nosy inside some of the city's most beautiful homes (don't we all?), you can sign up for an interiors tour (psmodsquad.com). It's a brilliant experience – Palm Springs' architectural masterpieces are simply extraordinary.

Built in the mid-century modern style, most of the houses are decorated in soft pastel shades and flaunt sharp angles. One of the greatest pleasures of this place is that nothing is taller than the palm trees that have become the true stars of the town, and no two houses are the same.

While you won't be dropping by Leonardo's for coffee, on the 90-minute Interiors Tour, you'll be taken inside three different homes, each is distinct and undeniably beautiful. If you're lucky, some of the homeowners will be there to answer questions and share stories. We took many of the design ideas we saw home with us – from the way one particular home hung their artwork to another's inspiring art deco furniture. It's just a shame we couldn't take their swimming pools too…

Take a look around the unique properties in Palm Springs

RECHARGE IN PALM SPRINGS

For spectacular views of the city, take a tram ride to the Mount San Jacinto State Park

GET YOUR SHOPPING KICK
Located a mere 20-minute drive away is Desert Hills Premium Outlets (premiumoutlets.com/deserthills). Here you can nab high-end fashion – home to Dolce & Gabbana, Saint Laurent, Jimmy Choo, Tory Burch and more – for up to 65% off. It pays to visit the website for promotions and grab a VIP Club coupon book for even more savings.

Tribal history
Climb aboard a jeep and hiking tour with Desert Adventures Red Jeep Tours (red-jeep.com) and learn about the landscape of Indian Canyons, the ancestral home of the Agua Caliente Band of Cahuilla Indians, where your knowledgeable guide will give you an introduction to the area's unique geological formations.

The Cahuilla Indian name for the Palm Springs area was Sec-he (boiling water), and the Spanish who later arrived named it Agua Caliente (hot water). Then came the name 'Palm Springs' in reference to both the native Washingtonia palm tree and the hot mineral springs on the tribal land. Today, remnants of the traditional Cahuilla society exist in the exquisite canyons that the tribe has worked to protect, while current tribal leaders work within the community to help strengthen and protect today's modern city.

All of the canyons – Murray, Andreas, Tahquitz, Chino and Palm – are beautiful and you can easily visit any one of them. Having found out we hadn't yet seen Elvis and Priscilla Presley's 'honeymoon hideaway', we made a quick pit stop before heading on to Andreas Canyon, situated just 10 minutes from downtown Palm Springs.

The walking tour is a gentle one-mile hike past hidden water caves and a multitude of palm trees – it's a must-do activity while in the area.

Natural beauty
Following a vertical climb of nearly 6,000ft, rotating all the way up, the Palm Springs Aerial Tramway comes to rest in Mount San Jacinto State Park. Here, you'll find a lofty sanctuary that offers 54 miles of diverse walking trails, with a captivating view into the Sonoran Desert below.

To take in the extraordinary varieties of desert plants, visit Moorten Botanical Garden. A living museum of desert lore, the garden has something for everyone, with glistening crystals, colourful rocks, ancient fossils, and pioneer and gold mining relics.

To see plants in their natural habitat, head north-east for an hour to visit the Joshua Tree National Park. A whopping 800,000 acres of desert, rock climbers know it as the best place to climb in California, while hikers seek out hidden, shady, desert-and-palm oases fed by natural springs and small streams.

When viewed from the roadside, the desert can seem bare. But explore on foot, bike or by jeep and you'll see blossoming wild flowers, scuttling lizards and the contorted trees for which the park was named. In springtime, the Joshua trees send up a huge single cream-coloured flower.

Heading home recharged
Back in the city, we spent our last afternoon, as any southern Californian should – in and around the hotel pool, cradling a cocktail. Then something quite remarkable happened. My husband, usually burning to move onto the next activity, was face down, fast asleep on a sun lounger.

If ever there was a resort designed to help you completely switch off and recharge, this is it.

GETTING THERE
✢ Go to visitpalmsprings.com or palmspringsca.gov for more on Palm Springs, including travel, hotels and a range of useful resources for visitors.

Feel well in WEST HOLLYWOOD

If you're after a fitness break, Helena Cartwright discovers that this small city in Los Angeles has a lot to offer the health-conscious traveller

We understand. You work hard on your fitness all year so the idea of a holiday where your Fitbit doesn't get much action isn't up there on your things to do. So, don't! Recently, fitness and holidays have consciously coupled. Wellness tourism has grown by 6.5%* annually over the past two years, more than twice as fast as tourism overall. But forget solo yoga trips and extreme juice detox retreats; head to sunny West Hollywood, or WeHo as it's affectionately known, for the best of both worlds.

The basics
Located at the base of the Hollywood Hills and adjacent to Beverly Hills, the city of West Hollywood is just 1.9 square miles in size. The city is comprised of three main districts: the world-famous Sunset Strip, Santa Monica Boulevard and the West Hollywood Design District.

Not to be confused with the more raucous Hollywood – home of the world-famous Walk of Fame – West Hollywood is where LA gets its healthy living reputation, featuring miles of idyllic hiking routes, plenty of opportunities to try the latest wellness trends and lots of charcoal lattes.

Getting around
Locals spend a good portion of their day driving around LA. But, given its small size, this is one of California's most walkable areas. Ride-sharing services can cover longer distances or help if you're in a rush to get to your meditation class (this is LA, after all).

Get active
Seasoned travellers will know that getting those legs moving is the only way to cure jet lag. If you're unfamiliar with the area, start with a guided tour. Bikes and Hikes LA offers a wealth of options. My husband and I chose the Celebrity Bike Tour, which was the perfect choice. It's an easy, stress-free tour as your guide highlights the area's landmarks and celebrity homes. I may or may not have spent an extra minute or two outside Leonardo DiCaprio's house.

Once you've got to grips with the area, head to the hills on your own. Runyon Canyon, with its stunning views and proximity to Hollywood, means it's

FEEL WELL IN WEST HOLLYWOOD

often full of stars and Instagrammers climbing their way to the top. The view is unrivalled. Downtown is spread out in front of you and the Hollywood sign sits just above, close enough for you to capture it on camera.

Another cracking spot to stretch your legs is Griffith Park. It's one of those places where you think you'll spend an hour or two, but happily end up staying for the day. Complete with an observatory and planetarium, you have access to more than 4,000 acres and 53 miles worth of hiking trails.

Sweat it out

Whatever the latest celebrity-approved fitness trend or wellness fad is this week, you'll find it started in West Hollywood. With five locations in California including a West Hollywood branch, Shape House has been an LA fixture for a few years now. Snuggle into a heated sleeping bag, switch on your favourite Netflix series (*Suits*, for me) and sweat out up to 800 calories as your body is heated to 70 degrees for 60 minutes.

I can't tell you it was painless. Halfway through, the dulcet sounds of Harvey Specter could no longer calm my racing heart. But an ice-cold flannel was laid across my head to see me through. People tend to go several times a month (or week) and I can see why. I had a massive adrenaline rush afterwards. Designed to burn calories, deepen sleep and improve skin, what more could you want?

Rest up at the Palihouse

And, relax

After exercise, comes the calm. Head to Unplug for meditation classes, which offer all the benefits of mindfulness with the added support of a guide. The sound healing classes, where you're urged to chant, will leave you happily rested. I left floating on a cloud saying, 'I could really get used to this way of life, you know?' over, and over, and over.

Food and drink

What's the point of working hard if you can't have some fun? EP & LP is a laid-back Asian-style lounge offering small plates designed for sharing. Head to the rooftop for the real deal, though. Overlooking the iconic skyline, the drinks are strong, the beats are heavy and as the night goes on the party gets louder.

For something a little quieter but equally as trendy, Conservatory, on Santa Monica Boulevard, has something for everyone. During the day, visit the street level café but at night, head upstairs to the first floor for a full bar and restaurant.

Take a hike

Santa Monica Pier

The afternoon is a great time to hit up the relaxed wellness food scene. Everywhere you look in California you'll see influences of Mexican cuisine. For the best (and healthiest), head to Gracias Madre. It came highly recommended by just about everyone we spoke to. It's 100% vegan friendly but its ingredients would fool even the fussiest of eaters. Pulled pork is replaced by barbecued jackfruit while cashew nacho cheese covers wheat tortillas, replicating both the taste and texture of the original dish.

Rest your tired legs

Palihouse West Hollywood is a boutique hotel just off Santa Monica Boulevard. It's quirky and eclectic but the rooms are incredibly spacious. Designed for longer stays, they're fitted with kitchens, living-dining spaces and marble-clad bathrooms. Most rooms have private terraces and all have drinks carts with miniature spirits, garnishes and recipe cards to help you rustle up drinks.

The rooftop bar is a haven for celeb-spotting too. When the weekend rolls around, you're pretty much guaranteed to spot a film star or five.

To the beach

Just 20 minutes from the coast, you can't holiday in West Hollywood without a visit to Santa Monica and nearby Malibu. Bike down the coast stopping just about wherever you fancy.

One thing you must do? Eat at Malibu Farm, based on the pier itself. It offers a farm-to-table menu with incredible views of the sea. Still a locally owned small business, despite its fast-growing popularity, it has delicious breakfasts, salads and sandwiches, which are ideal to satisfy that post-cycle hunger.

GETTING THERE

✢ Head to visitwesthollywood.com or www.weho.org for more information. For Palihouse West Hollywood, visit www.palisociety.com for more information or availability and bookings.

A natural WONDER

With its giant rock faces, jagged peaks and thundering waterfalls, Yosemite National Park is one of the world's most iconic sights. When we're finally allowed to explore the world again, it deserves a place on all our bucket lists...

Even the most jaded traveller will look past the crowds in amazement when wandering the trails below the towering canyon walls of Yosemite National Park. **The breathtaking landmark has the ability to amaze, surprise and charm in equal measure.** Established in October 1890 as one of the first national parks, the protected territory encompasses 1,200 square miles of scenic wild lands in the Sierra Nevada, ranging hugely in height above sea level from 2,000-12,000ft!

Approximately four million people visit each year, most during the summer, but Yosemite offers adventure all year round. My husband Mitul and I visited the park in September, and we hiked in relative peace. The weather was cool in the mornings, but a perfect 20C later in the day.

The highlights

Half Dome is Yosemite's most distinctive natural monument. An impressive 87 million years old and with a 93 per cent vertical grade, it's the sheerest cliff in North America. Climbers come from all over the world to tackle its legendary north face, but good hikers can reach the summit, too, via a 17-mile round trip.

Yosemite's waterfalls are mesmerising, especially when the spring run-off turns them into spectacularly thunderous cataracts. Yosemite Falls is considered among the tallest waterfalls in North America, dropping 2,425ft in three tiers. Bridalveil, Vernal and Nevada Falls are also nearby.

For the best photo opportunity, head to Tunnel View, made famous by landscape photographer Ansel Adams. It's one of the best places in the park to capture El Capitan, Half Dome and Bridalveil Fall all in the same shot.

For another great photo, Glacier Point, located 3,214ft above the valley floor, has one of the most commanding views in the whole state of California. You'll find the entire Eastern Yosemite Valley spread out before you, from Yosemite Falls to Half Dome, practically looming at eye level. If you look closely, you'll be able to spot hikes on its summit. To the right of Half Dome, you'll find the wavy, white ribbons of Nevada Falls and Vernal Falls.

Head to the heart

The heart of the park is Yosemite Valley. There's one road that loops through it, linking car parks and villages to the hiking trails and viewpoints. If you drive this loop (or take the Yosemite Shuttle) you can see almost half of the park's

A NATURAL WONDER

iconic landmarks: the giant rock wall of El Capitan, the granite bust of Half Dome and North America's highest waterfall, Yosemite Falls. Getting to them all, however, requires a hike.

For the fullest experience of Yosemite National Park, park your car and get on the trails. Whether you're looking for rigorous hikes or a leisurely saunter through shaded forest paths, there's a trail for all abilities. Chances are you're only a stone's throw away from one at any time. These are our favourites…

✢ VALLEY LOOP TRAIL
11.5 or 7.2 miles
See all of the Yosemite Valley highlights – but none of its crowds – on this loop with views of El Capitan, Yosemite Falls, Sentinel Rock, Bridalveil Fall and the Merced River. Start the 11.5-mile loop at Lower Yosemite Fall and go in either direction. For the 7.2-mile half loop, take the spur trail to cross the Merced at El Capitan Bridge.

✢ MIST TRAIL
1.2 miles with an option to extend
Perhaps Yosemite's most popular path, it deserves all the attention it attracts. The trail brings you in close proximity to two major waterfalls: Vernal Falls and Nevada Falls. Hike 1.2 miles (one-way) and a vertical 1,000ft to the top of Vernal Falls. Going to Nevada Falls adds 1.5 miles and 1,000ft to your trip. At the top of the falls the view is a little scary – but jaw-dropping nonetheless.

Vernal Falls

✢ MIRROR LAKE LOOP
2 or 7 miles
From the nearby shuttle stop, a one-mile paved road leads to Mirror Lake, the shallow body of water that gives this trail its name. The lake reflects the already spectacular views of Tenaya Canyon and the ubiquitous Half Dome. Visit in spring or early summer, as the lake gradually dries out, often existing as a meadow from late summer. You can, if you wish, make a five-mile loop around the lake / meadow, following Tenaya Creek.

✢ FOUR-MILE TRAIL
4.8 miles
The elevation change on this steep trail from Glacier Point is a whopping 3,200ft – but it's all downhill. As you descend, take in views of Yosemite Valley, including Half Dome. Take the hiker shuttle to the trailhead.

Helena and Mitul

Wonderful wildlife

Yosemite is home to many species of wildlife, including American black bears, majestic great grey owls, plucky marmots, tiny pikas and much, much more. Seeing any of these animals in their natural habitat is an unforgettable experience, but make sure you help protect them. Firstly, drive slowly: bears and other wildlife are often spotted crossing the roads, and you're more likely to spot them if you're not speeding. Secondly, never approach or feed them. Lastly, if you're staying on-site, always use a bear-proof food locker when camping. Yosemite bears are clever and are often found rummaging for food, which is harmful to them.

Santa Monica Pier

Time to rest and relax

There are campsites, lodges and hotels within the park, but for something really special head to the comforts of Tenaya Lodge at Yosemite, just two miles outside the park. After a long day hiking, you can relax and unwind with a massage at the spa, enjoy dinner in the on-site restaurant and kick back under the stars with some sticky marshmallow s'mores. You can book a variety of activities based on the seasons.

Other activites

✢ HOP ON A BIKE
One of the best ways to see the valley floor is by bike. Within Yosemite, there are 12 miles of designated bike trails in the eastern end of the valley, so jump into the saddle and go!

✢ GO ZIPLINING
The Yosemite Zipline and Adventure Ranch in Mariposa offers six different courses. It's exhilarating, with great guides.

✢ GIVE YOUR FEET A REST
Take a tour in an open-air tram. It's approximately 2 hours long and is led by a knowledgeable ranger. You'll get to see all the highlights as you learn about the history, flora, and fauna throughout the park.

GETTING THERE

✢ **A park pass for Yosemite National Park is valid for seven consecutive days, giving you time to explore properly**

✢ **Fly from the UK to San Francisco. Yosemite is approximately 200 miles east, so you could hire a car and pack in a classic Californian road trip experience too**

Magical MEXICO

Whale-watching, tequila-tasting and golden sands – welcome to Puerto Vallarta

As the last rays of sun glimmer on the ocean, two enormous fins break the surface of the water. A mother and calf humpback whale dive gracefully into the deep as the sun sets on another day in the paradise of Puerto Vallarta.

Nestled snugly within Banderas Bay, here the unending stretches of golden sand beaches are lapped by the warm waters of the Pacific Ocean. Once a small, sleepy fishing village, the past 50 years have seen this town bloom into a bustling hub of gastronomy and artistic charm.

Sheltered from storms by the jungle-clad Sierra Nevada Mountains, Puerto Vallarta enjoys over 300 gloriously sunny days a year. On warm, balmy evenings you'll find streets buzzing with live music and artisanal marketplaces. Whether you're a couple planning a romantic getaway, a solo traveller looking to make new friends or a family seeking the trip of a lifetime, it's easy to fall in love with this warm, welcoming and colourful town. It's perfect for a recharging break.

MAGICAL MEXICO

Luxurious Casa Kimberly, once home to Elizabeth Taylor and Richard Burton

Puerto Vallarta's secrets and surprises

Ambling through the picturesque Romantic Zone, our local guide was keen to dish the dirt on the celebrity romance that caught the world's attention in the Sixties. In 1964 Puerto Vallarta starred as the location for Elizabeth Taylor and Richard Burton's Hollywood film *The Night of the Iguana*. The couple were in the midst of a scandalous affair – though madly in love, both were married to other people. Burton and Taylor's not-so-secret affair was fraught with turbulent fights, but they brought fame to the area as a glamorous getaway for decades to come. You can even stay in the iconic red clay-roofed house the Hollywood stars once called home – now known as Casa Kimberly, the luxurious property boasts panoramic views over Banderas Bay.

This is the perfect destination to slow down and explore on foot – we found charming surprises around every corner. Leafy plazas glint with elegant mosaics, and chocolate shops create melt-in-the-mouth sweet treats with local cacao. Both traditional and modern festivals ignite the streets with costumed parades and dances, including an eight-day annual celebration of Pride in this proudly LGBTQ-friendly holiday destination.

A stroll down the Malecón boardwalk reveals a burgeoning art scene. On a free guided art tour, I was enchanted by the sculptures designed to be climbed on. I'd never have guessed that I would end up scaling a towering ladder up to the sky, clambering atop a majestic seahorse looking out to sea, or reclining on an otherworldly brass throne created by local artists. But that's the way of life in Puerto Vallarta; children and adults alike are encouraged to embrace their playful side. >>

"Everyone is encouraged to embrace their playful side"

MINDFUL TRAVEL | 93

Vallarta Botanical Gardens is a delight for nature lovers

Out on the waves

Banderas Bay provides a safe haven for a kaleidoscope of tropical marine life, and it's where bottlenose dolphins, humpback whales and sea turtles come to breed and raise their young.

You'll often spot them from the shore, but for a close-up look, your best bet is a boat tour. For an adventurous and utterly glamorous day out, hop aboard a luxury yacht and glide across glittering waves to the very best snorkelling areas, where coral reefs teem with a rainbow of fish. Many boats are equipped with a full bar – so you can unwind on deck with an ice-cold margarita while humpbacks surface nearby.

Conserving natural beauty at the Vallarta Botanical Gardens

Even in the centre of town we were never far from nature – chirruping birds glide overhead, lush tropical trees line the streets and the ocean sparkles on the horizon. But if, like me, you are a lover of the great outdoors, there is no better way to reconnect with nature than a visit to the Vallarta Botanical Gardens. Here the local guides are true experts in what they do, cultivating and conserving 80 acres of land in the extraordinarily biodiverse Sierra Madre mountains.

A culinary tour through the grounds was illuminating and delicious; we sampled sugary hibiscus flowers, sweet cinnamon sticks carved from tree bark and the potent, miniscule seeds of vanilla pods plucked from rare orchids.

Lunch here was also suitably idyllic. On a balcony overlooking rustling treetops, with hummingbirds darting across our table, we were served a meal of rich, authentic Mexican cuisine made with ingredients sourced from the reserve itself. The vanilla ice cream was unlike anything I've ever tasted.

Downstairs there are art exhibitions and artisanal wares made by local indigenous artists who have crafted and hand-painted everything from glossy ceramic bowls to colourful maracas made from dried fruits. Needless to say, I came home laden with enough gifts to fill a whole suitcase.

> "It's a safe haven for a kaleidoscope of tropical marine life"

MAGICAL MEXICO

Cooking up a storm

Speak to any local and they'll tell you the sound of an authentic Mexican restaurant is clapping. How so? Properly prepared corn tortillas must be patted between the hands, rounded into soft circles before they are flattened and cooked. These warm delights can then be piled high with any number of delicious fillings – in Puerto Vallarta, seafood is a popular choice for its zingy freshness, while my personal favourite was creamy guacamole, spicy mixed vegetables and queso fresco cheese.

A cooking class proved a great way to learn about the traditional techniques and generations-old recipes behind classic Mexican dishes. At Gaby's restaurant we prepared an impressive range of salsas, mains and even a local dessert, all on a shady roof terrace overlooking the sun-soaked splendour of the town.

Sampling local brews

From rustic, hole-in-the-wall spots where locals gather over icy cold beers, to glitzy open-air bars decked out with shimmering dance floors, Puerto Vallarta is home to a hotchpotch of wonderful places to enjoy a drink. Part of the charm here is that you'll always be an easy stroll away from your next location, and there is no shortage of delicious beverages.

The beachfront city is located in Jalisco – for tequila to be deemed authentic, it must be produced within this state. As such, we found an incredible array of tequilas, each with its own unique blend of warmly spiced flavours. Raicilla is another regional delicacy – described proudly by locals as Mexican moonshine, this deep, smoky spirit packs a punch that leaves you invigorated yet relaxed.

Try either in a chilled cocktail made with fresh fruits, or drink the spirits straight, like the locals, for a more authentic (and fiery!) experience. We knocked back a fair few of these shots on our final evening, while dancing to Latin music at a buzzing neighbourhood bar until the small hours.

Though we felt a little sore on the flight home, it was the perfect end to a week spent in pure, tropical bliss.

"Each tequila has its own unique blend of spiced flavours"

Overlooking Banderas Bay, the beachfront city is home to an incredible array of tequilas

MINDFUL TRAVEL | 95

PARADISE
islands

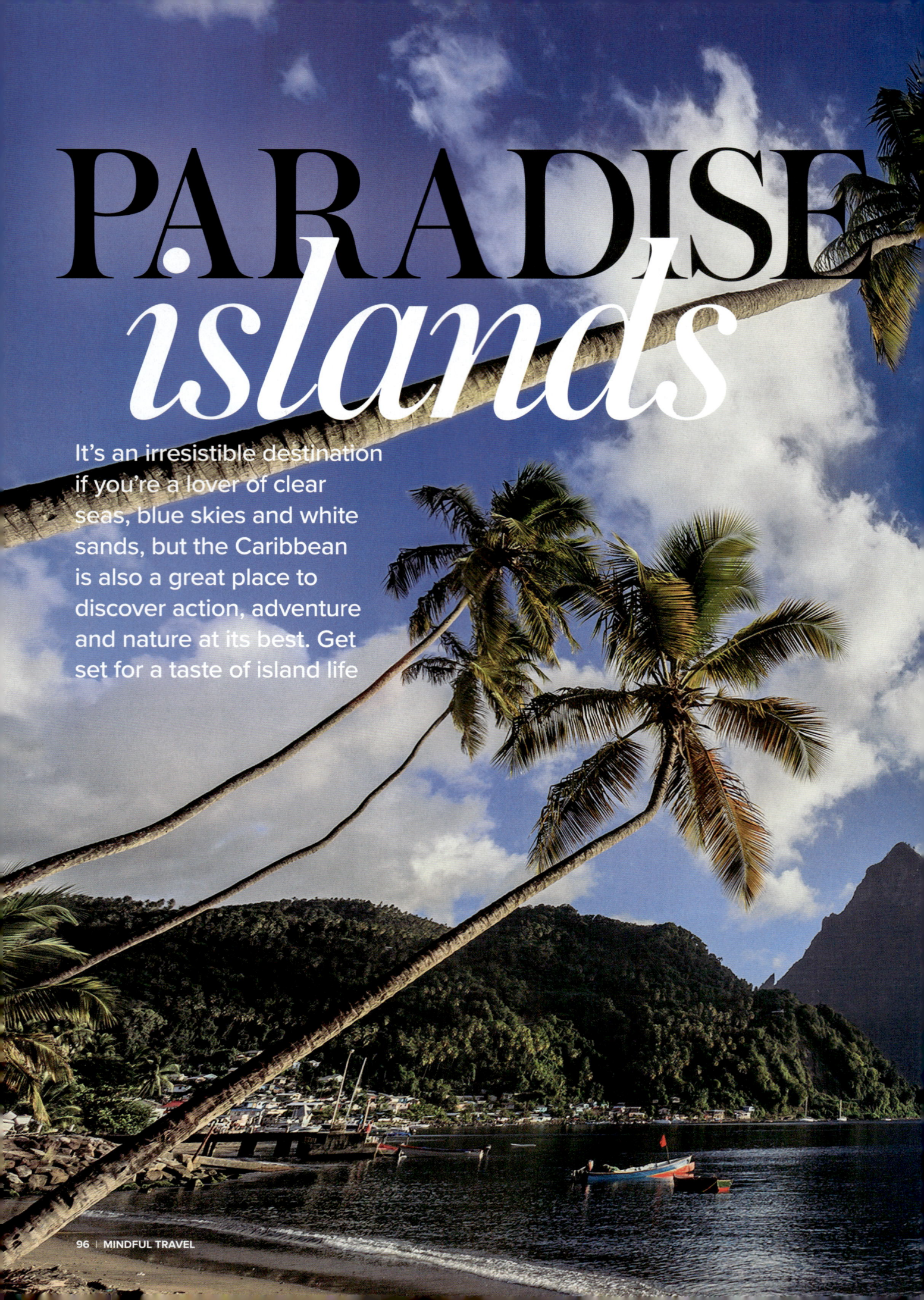

It's an irresistible destination if you're a lover of clear seas, blue skies and white sands, but the Caribbean is also a great place to discover action, adventure and nature at its best. Get set for a taste of island life

PARADISE ISLAND

In love with St Lucia

Best known as a honeymoon hotspot, the island is also perfect for a mother and daughter adventure, discovers Tanya Pearey. Walking to the airport departure gate, it felt as if we were about to board an ark – everyone was in pairs because St Lucia is hugely popular with newlyweds. But arriving at our suite at the Marigot Bay Resort, in the north west of the island, my daughter Savannah and I were looking for a lively adventure break, packed with activities. Did we find it?

The answer is an emphatic yes, and we began by discovering that St Lucia's beautifully rugged and mountainous landscape is perfect for walking – as long as you avoid the heat of the day and take plenty of water.

We tackled Marigot Bay's Ridge Walk, a steady 45-minute uphill climb under tree cover, rewarded at the top by heady views overlooking the bay and resort – and, with the help of binoculars, the neighbouring island of Martinique to the north.

For less effort, try the Tet Paul Nature Trail. It's a manageable, flat 45-minute stroll, offering great views of Jalousie Bay and Gros Piton – the larger of the island's two volcanic peaks, which rise majestically from the clear blue waters.

You'll get uninterrupted views of both spikes if you head for lunch at Jade Mountain Club. The open-air restaurant there has views across the Caribbean Sea to the Pitons that are picture-perfect.

A more high-octane way to grab a glimpse of the Pitons comes while zip-wiring at Morne Coubaril. We spent an hour zipping through the exotic canopy of coconut, mango and banyan trees, and across a bamboo-fringed gorge, on eight different cables – exhilarating!

Of course you can't come to St Lucia without getting on the water, so we hired a double kayak and were led by a guide along the coast past a banana plantation, and into the next cove.

Here we dragged our kayaks across a few yards of sand into the tranquil waterway of the Roseau River where we paddled past overgrown sugar cane plantations. Back at the resort we went straight to the spa – an oasis of calm.

The balmy climate, exotic landscape and golden-sanded beaches make St Lucia the perfect romantic destination. But you don't have to be a loved-up couple to make the most of this Caribbean paradise. 'Fancy watching the sunset over the sea with a rum cocktail?' I asked Savannah. 'I do!' she said. >>

Need to know
✣ **Prices for a Resort View Junior Suite at Marigot Bay Resort and Marina include breakfast but exclude 10% tax and 10% service charge. Visit marigotbayresort.com or call +1 758 458 5300. For more info about St Lucia, visit stlucia.org**

Tanya and Savannah preparing to zip-wire. *Left:* Marigot Bay Resort

PERFECT FOR Activities

Get happy in Aruba

White sand, turquoise water and a chance to chill? Yes please, says Jane Druker.

Aruba is known as 'One Happy Island' – and it lives up to its name. It's just 21 miles long, so everything is nearby. From the airport it's a mere 15-minute ride to the Aruba Marriott Resort & Casino, a giant hotel with multiple pools, for families as well as adults only, a stunning beachside, said casino and many restaurants. Arriving at dinner after a swift shower and change of outfit, I pottered down to the beachside location and sat at a table on the beach, feet bathed in warm sand, Sauvignon in hand, watching the sun go down and eating local red snapper – could there be a more decadent, beautiful moment?

There was a switch of gear in the morning as I roared off on a private jeep tour of a National Park. I'd assumed it would be a leisurely ride around the island – but this was off-road driving, flying up and barrelling down the rocky terrain. Scary, but exhilarating too. I especially loved a magical morning spent learning to meditate at a local butterfly farm, where the enclosure danced with bright, jewel-coloured butterflies. As our meditation teacher, Shanty, guided us through both a sitting meditation, something utterly special happened – various butterflies landed on my hair, my head and my hands. This is considered very lucky according to Shanty, and I had to make a wish each time.

This island is great for families, couples and, well, everyone except real bah humbugs. I certainly didn't want to leave, and returned recharged and with new skills designed to keep me happy and healthy long after.

PERFECT FOR Relaxation

Top left: Flamingo beach. *Top:* Aruba Marriott Resort. *Above:* Jane meditating. *Below:* Colonial Dutch architecture in capital Oranjestad

Need to know
✢ Flights to Aruba return with KLM.com (prices dependent on time of year). Stays at Aruba Marriott Hotel & Casino (marriothotels.com). For more details, visit aruba.com

PARADISE ISLAND

Can I take him home?

During an extraordinary visit to the Bahamas, Zoe West met some VIPs with a difference.

It was my first child-free holiday in 10 years, and the last thing I expected was to find myself paddling with pigs in the Bahamas. Yet here I was frolicking around in turquoise waters with Ginger and Wilbur.

Swimming with pigs is an experience that regularly features on travel bucket lists, and I soon found out why. There really is nothing more joyous than seeing these adorable pigs bobbing in the undulating waves with snouts in the air.

No one really knows exactly how the pigs came to be on these lush tropical islands – they're certainly not native. But the story the locals tell is they were shipwrecked nearby and then swam to shore. Not the worst place to be stranded…

The more famous wild swimming pigs of the Bahamas can be found on the Exuma Islands, a two-hour boat ride from where I was staying in the capital, Nassau. I opted for a 'closer to home' experience on Rose Island, a mere 25-minute boat ride away.

It's a surreal experience to be floating about in the crystal clear waters alongside a pig who seems to be enjoying itself as much as you – and that fun is contagious. Pigs aside, this tropical oasis is the perfect playground. There's snorkelling, beach volleyball and kayaking, and of course a relaxed beach bar where sipping a piña colada or two is a Bahamian must. The island is also a sanctuary to protected wildlife, including royal peacocks, curly tailed-lizards and wonderful ocean reef life.

Back in Nassau, the newly opened Grand Hyatt Hotel forms part of the impressive Baha Mar resort on beautiful Cable Beach. From here, you can head for the biggest casino on the island, watch resident flamingos, gaze at sharks and sea turtles at the poolside aquarium or dine at one of many astounding restaurants.

With 700 islands, the Bahamas is a special place, and the moments spent on my balcony watching the sun rise over incredibly photogenic turquoise waters were just perfect. Next time I'll simply have to take the kids because, unfortunately, I wasn't allowed to bring a swimming pig home. >>

PERFECT FOR Wildlife

Top and left: Exuma Islands. *Above:* Zoe on Rose Island with a swimming pig

Need to know
✢ BA Holidays offer a nine-hour direct flight from London to Lynden Pindling International Airport, Nassau. Visit bahamar.com. The Sandy Toes trip to Rose Island is available for both adults and kids; happily children 0-3 years go free.

Idyllic Dominican Republic

This lush island paradise boasts 250 miles of the world's top beaches, but Rose Fooks has her own favourites.

The most idyllic beach you can imagine really does exist, and it's waiting at Playa Juanillo in the Dominican Republic. Calmly rippling, the ocean's colour mirrors the cloudless sky, with palm trees creating a dappled shade on the white sand.

Arriving at Cap Cana, the most exclusive part of the island, we slowly meandered, each with a glass of delicious sangria, into the warm shallows, feeling like the luckiest people in the world to have discovered an idyllic heaven that's just 10 minutes from the airport.

The Dominican Republic was colonised by Spain in 1492, and although it's now independent, the Spanish influence is still apparent in its language and cuisine.

The Grand Palladium Palace Resort and Spa, a hotel within a larger resort of five hotels, is perfect for exploring the island's picturesque coastline. From here you're free to roam over almost 2km of one of the island's most iconic Atlantic beaches, Bávaro Beach in Punta Cana.

This all-inclusive resort is brilliant for families — its kids club is open from 9am to 11pm, with activities including zip line and costumed television characters. And this resort is so vast that you could spend a week here and discover a new restaurant, bar and pool every day.

It's essential to try the chocolate tasting experience at Chocolate & CIA. Cocoa is one of the main exports from the island and is considered some of the highest quality in the world — I can verify it's exceptionally good. I hope to head back soon, not just for the blissful beaches — but to restock on chocolate.

Need to know
✢ **A one-night stay in a Junior Suite Swim Up at Grand Palladium Palace Resort Spa & Casino is all-inclusive, based on two people sharing. BA flies to Santo Domingo or Punta Cana from Gatwick; TUI flies from Manchester and Gatwick to Punta Cana and Puerto Plata.**

Above: **Juanillo Beach.** *Right and below:* **The Grand Palladium Palace Resort and Spa**

PERFECT FOR Families

PARADISE ISLAND

Chilling in Jamaica

The beach resort of Negril made a great base for Catherine Westwood's family to explore and relax.

Azure sky, turquoise sea and powder-soft sand? Check. Situated in Negril, on the west coast, Seven Mile Beach is a dream to visit and home to the Beaches Resort, where breakfasts are cooked to order at the beachfront restaurant. From open-air massages to kayaking and snorkelling, there's something for everyone here.

Located on the beautiful Seven Mile Beach, Beaches Negril Resort & Spa all-inclusive resort is totally about enjoying the water, with six pools, three hot tubs and a special kids' canopy pool. Guest rooms have dark wooden furnishings and four-poster beds – all with Caribbean flair. The overall feel is one of true relaxation.

About an hour from Negril is Chukka, home to lots of outdoor activities, including quad biking, zip-lining and horse riding. The horses are stabled in an idyllic location overlooking the ocean, which even comes complete with a sea swing. You don't need lots of riding experience – just pay attention to the guide's instructions and follow the leader. The land trips cover the local area from river beds to scenic hill climbs, and take in plenty of stunning scenery. The kids will love it.

There is also another way to see Jamaica – from the sea. One of the best options is to take the Island Routes Reggae Family Catamaran, which departs from the shore at Beaches Negril. Dive off the boat into the crystal clear warm waters and snorkel over the reefs that are home to many vibrant tropical fish, sea urchins and starfish.

Need to know
✢ **A seven-night stay at Beaches Negril Resort & Spa in a Grande Luxe King Room includes luxury (all-inclusive) accommodation, as well as return economy flights with Virgin Atlantic from London Gatwick and resort transfers. Visit beaches.co.uk/resorts/negril to find out more**

PERFECT FOR Exploring

Above left: Beaches Negril Resort & Spa. *Above right:* A local fruit stand in Ocho Rios. *Bottom right:* Rick's Cafe, Negril

Wild wellness in MAURITIUS

Yoga on the beach, meditation by a stream and a mindful walk through a tropical rainforest... Tanya Pearey visits an island gem in the Indian Ocean

The waves crash on the distant coral reef. A gentle breeze fans my face. Above, I can hear the sound of rustling palm leaves. Below, I can feel the soft warm sand between my toes. Looking out to sea, I watch the evening sun slip below a shimmering aqua horizon.

"And reeelaaax…" breathes my yoga teacher Karine Kleb. It's not difficult. I've never felt so calm in my life. Yoga in Witham village hall on a wet Wednesday will never be the same again!

To be honest, none of my relaxation experiences will ever be the same again after a trip to Heritage Le Telfair. Located at the beach edge of Bel Ombre, a village in the less developed south of the island, this top wellness resort in Mauritius has a focus on wellness out in the open. And what a tranquil and stunning "open" it is.

A tropical paradise

Mauritius has long been a top destination for honeymooners. The volcanic island is 1,200 miles from the south-east coast of Africa and enjoys year-long warm temperatures. Its 200 miles of pristine-white sandy beaches are fringed by palm trees and ringed by one of the longest unbroken barrier reefs in the world, which makes the sea crystal clear and calm to swim in.

But the African country also has imposing mountains and dramatic rainforests (plus a delicious and healthy fusion-food culture), making it the perfect natural spot to decompress.

Le Telfair was renovated in the summer of 2017 and now it hosts what it hopes will become annual Wellness Festivals. Activities, led by wellness gurus from around the globe, which will take place at the resort and at a variety of nearby outdoor venues, including iconic natural landmarks such as the Le Morne peninsula, a UNESCO World Heritage site.

Walk on the wild side

Heritage Le Telfair, though, runs a weekly programme of free feel-good activities throughout the year – from cookery demos to wellness walks – that make the most of this idyllic location. The week I am here they've flown in yoga expert Karine from her home in France to lead twice-daily sessions. I also join a group walk through a nearby rainforest for a spot of "forest bathing". We drive a few minutes from the hotel but remain on the resort grounds. The site used to be a sugar plantation and

WILD WELLNESS IN MAURITIUS

spans a vast 2,500 hectares. In addition to the hotel area (with its three pools and 12 restaurants and bars spread along the beachside), there's a huge villa complex, 12-hole golf course and 19th-century chateau – where you can stay upstairs in the exclusive four-poster bedroomed apartment or dine below in the top-end restaurant. It has a menu with signature dishes by the Michelin-starred chef David Toutain. We head for the many hectares of untouched hilly rainforest to begin our walk by a bubbling stream. We sit here, in yoga pose, meditating for five minutes before our "mindful" stroll begins.

Natural beauty

It's hard not to feel refreshed by a walk where you are so immersed in the natural world – the sound of birdsong and the bubbling water is instantly relaxing. The views of rainforested hills are lush variations of green – just looking at them makes you feel glad to be alive. We pass a tree hung with large fruit bats, disturb a mother and baby deer who skip off together down a gorge, and marvel at a small troupe of monkeys as they scatter on the track ahead of us. We hike up to a nearby waterfall, discarding shoes and socks for a reinvigorating paddle.

And relax...

Back at the hotel's spa it's the natural environment that they're trying to recreate – with splashes of greenery and bubbling water features. And it works. I feel super relaxed for my massage and Ohashiatsu treatments.

I'm dressed in a judo-style outfit, lying on matting on the floor while my Ohashiatsu therapist moves my body around and applies pressure to relax and restore me. "The practitioner gets as much out of the treatment as the receiver," he tells me afterwards. Then chastises me for not letting myself chill sufficiently at the start!

Off-site exploring

The next day there's no pressure – to relax or do anything other than enjoy – when we assemble for a half-day trip around the local area, courtesy of tour company Mautourco (mautourco.com). We learn how most locals earn a living as we watch skilled fishermen bring their catch of red snapper onto the beach to sell to the local fishmonger. We hear about nearby shipwrecks and the history of the sugar plantations, and take in the truly breathtaking costal views at Macondé, a rocky outcrop at the Baie du Cap, and the deserted beach nearby.

We visit prominent tourist attractions, including the Seven Coloured Earths – a geological formation of rainbow volcanic rock – and the Chamarel Rum Distillery, to celebrate the drink of choice in these parts.

The island's national airline, Air Mauritius, has recently upgraded its fleet with the brand-new Airbus A330-900neo, which offers state-of-the-art entertainment, including WiFi, with advanced lighting and air management in all cabins, and flat-bed seating in Business Class. This, they say, will ensure travellers "arrive refreshed and ready to enjoy...". No worries if not, though, as you can't help but relax and recharge as soon as you step outside on this glorious island.

Relax in the hotel's spa

Yoga on the beach – bliss!

The Garden View Suite at Heritage Le Telfair

Need to know
✢ Rates at the Heritage Le Telfair resort are based on two sharing a Garden View Suite on a bed & breakfast basis.
✢ Wellness Bliss packages include a consultation and creation of a personal programme of treatments, activities and eating plan, featuring one wellness experience a day from a range of options.
✢ For more information, visit heritageresorts.mu For reservations, email resa@heritageresorts.mu
✢ Air Mauritius is the only airline to fly direct non-stop from London Heathrow to Mauritius. Look out for special fares that are offered from time to time. For more information, visit airmauritius.com or call 020 7434 4375.

Breathtaking CAMBODIA

A trip to Vietnam's Mekong Delta and Cambodia's luxury island retreats and famous temples has to be on your bucket list (eventually). Here's why…

As one of the seven wonders of the world, Angkor Wat – the City of Temples – is undoubtedly the highlight of a trip but lush, green Cambodia is packed with other gems, too, from bird reserves where you feel as if time stands still to romantic palm-fringed coastlines, impeccable hotels with smiley staff and zippy cities with neon lights and cocktail bars. Weather-wise, it's best to go from November to April, outside those times the rain leads to the seasonal flooding its farmers need to grow rice.

Take in the Mekong Delta

It's worth starting your journey in Vietnam's Mekong Delta. The low-lying flood plain, ideal for rice-growing, is packed with bustling family businesses and craft enterprises whose owners delight in welcoming tourists. Visiting in late January, the skies are blue and it's sunny and warm. People outdoors and working in fields sport the familiar pointed circular hats, called non la, which are woven from palm or bamboo.

Strolling into the leafy jungle, intersected with mud-brown tributaries, I was about to be shown how people work and live. As we navigated the river in a flat-bottomed boat, snakes and crocs sprang to mind but our cheery guide Mr Doan said not to worry. 'If there was anything living here it would be eaten – the Vietnamese eat everything!' Reassured and doubling up on mosquito

104 | MINDFUL TRAVEL

BREATHTAKING CAMBODIA

Locals head to market in flat-bottomed boats; at sunset, the island is bathed in a pink glow

"Island boardwalks meander through lush vegetation revealing unspoilt hideaway coves where you can swim and snorkel"

repellent, I learnt how to make rice noodles in a basic outdoor warehouse. Nothing goes to waste – even rice husks are used to keep the oven fires burning. Next stop, in a simple, stylish restaurant kitchen, I tried my hand at banh xeo (pancakes) with rice flour and coconut milk – making them was fun, eating them even better. Next, we met Mr Nguyen Cuong and his family, Grandma resting in a hammock. He replanted his family's longan and lychee crop with jelly leaf vines to make a Vietnamese jelly dessert – it's hugely popular, though it's an acquired taste. On our last visit, a Vietnamese family in a charming peppermint green house welcomed us into their home to have honey tea made with a herb leaf and kumquat – their 10-year-old daughter speaks near-perfect English, despite never having left the Mekong Delta.

The Can Tho Ecolodge in the Ben Tre province, a calm oasis of eco-style luxury on the banks of the Can Tho river, avoids plastic and supports green initiatives. Request an early breakfast and head out by boat to the Cai Rang floating market, where wholesalers ply their trade from boats laden with fruit and veg from orchards and farms further up the river. Hungry? Takeaway vendors in motorboats will chug up with sweet Vietnamese coffee, banh mi (baguette) snacks or beautifully sculpted, ready-to-eat juicy pineapples, all sold for a few dong (elsewhere though dollars are your easiest currency).

It's a taste of Vietnam to savour – and see sooner rather than later. With the threat of climate change and rising sea levels, the Mekong Delta is likely to be flooded in just 10 years' time unless preventative measures succeed in saving it.

Boarding our minibus, complete with faux silk, gold tasselled curtains and drapes that adorn every coach here, it's a four- to five-hour drive across the Ha Tien border and into Cambodia. Here, the wooden houses are open-fronted like the Vietnamese style homes and shops but, significantly, they are raised >>

Buddhist monks at Angkor Wat, the 'Temple City'; *below*, the local cuisine

on high stilts. It's instantly greener and hillier, too, with colourful flowering shrubs and striking palmyra trees silhouetted against blue skies. Hammocks are slung in shady spots everywhere, in front yards, cafes and tuk-tuks. For a dollar apiece you can enjoy a refreshing takeaway coconut water in green coconuts

Enjoy sunset cocktails

An hour from the border on the southwest coast is the small seaside resort of Kep, which has a fresher than fresh crab market where fishermen haul baskets of crabs from the sea to the stalls. Here the water's edge is tatty and workaday, yet just minutes up the coast you'll find clear water and pristine sandy beaches dotted with palms. Once feted as Cambodia's riviera in the 60s, Kep's bourgeois appeal was anathema to the Khmer Rouge, who took the country into its dark age in the 70s. To this day, former King Sihanouk's modernist villa lies decaying, its walls pocked with bullet holes.

Like much of Cambodia, Kep looks to the future and not the past — and at The Sailing Club Bar & Restaurant sunset cocktails are the order of the day. This is a family-friendly, relaxed place to sink a sundowner. Its pier stretches way out into the shallow water and (for a fee of around $400 or so) you can even book a private champagne supper for two for a special occasion.

The Samanea Beach Resort, with gardens, mountain views and an infinity pier fading to a point in the distant blue sea, is a romantic sunset location. The rooms are stylish and very comfortable, with a divine outdoor bathroom. Its restaurant, which is open to the garden, offers a blend of Khmer and French cuisine (Cambodia was a protectorate of France from 1863 until 1953). The crab amok is superb. Fish amok is Cambodia's national dish, a curry made with chillies, lemongrass, kaffir lime, palm sugar and coconut, and served in a banana leaf bowl. Delicious.

Birdwatching and pepper tasting

To see a conservation project in its early stages, visit the Anlung Pring bird reserve in Kampot, a community-led initiative supported by Birdlife International. The long dirt track out will challenge your suspension but the reward is seeing, among others, the world's tallest flying bird — the sarus crane, which visits from December until April. And gastronomes will love a day at La Plantation in Kampot, a social enterprise that employs local people on fair wages while producing the world's finest organic pepper. You'll tour the pepper fields, then try a tasting session. Rather like wine tasting you inhale the aroma first, then taste and make notes. Stock up on peppers, salt and spices as well as local handicrafts, including beautiful plant-dyed, hand-woven scarves. Not only are the prices low but a percentage of the profits supports local school children.

Stay in a luxury island hideaway

Six Senses Koh Krabey Island is a slice of paradise Cambodia-style. From the super-smart mainland reception, there's a glamorous 15-minute speedboat ride to the island, where Six Senses has 40 contemporary villas nestled in limestone hills clad with lush vegetation and banyan trees. With floor-to-ceiling windows, you feel at one with nature outdoors yet each villa is completely

Relax at Six Senses Krabey Island; right, pepper plantation; below, snorkelling

private, with its own keyhole views of paradise, an outdoor deck area and a personal pool. Electric buggies are on hand 24 hours a day, and boardwalk routes meander through the vegetation revealing unspoilt hideaway coves where you can swim and snorkel, plus there's a large infinity pool. Relaxation and wellbeing are what this island is all about, so bliss out with a heavenly spa treatment and make your own massage oil and foot scrub.

Leaving this tranquil paradise was hard but it's not the only luxury island on offer. Alila Villas on the neighbouring island of Koh Russey is a stylish, minimalist resort with fabulous beachfront restaurants, and a honeymoon-worthy sandy beach that stretches out to the sparkling ocean. It's around a 10-minute drive from Sihanoukville Airport and three to four hours from Kampot.

Siem Reap and the temples

Siem Reap, a one-hour flight from Sihanoukville, has a population of half a million and a plethora of elegant hotels, restaurants and shops where you can pick up brands like Nike at very good prices (lots of designer clothing is actually made in Cambodia).

Exploring the market and checking out cocktail bars like Miss Wong is de rigueur but watch out for the anarchic traffic — tuk-tuks, scooters, cars and bikes career with wild abandon — if you're on wheels in Cambodia, anything goes! Having a few words of Khmer delights anyone you meet, and liberal use of 'Sues'day' (hello) and 'Awkuhn' (thank you) will elicit smiles everywhere.

For an oasis of calm in the centre of the city, the Khmer-style, luxurious Montra Nivesha hotel is a must. In true boutique hotel style, there's a lush garden with two pools and a spa, and the spacious rooms showcase Cambodian arts and crafts. Meals are exquisitely presented and delicious. From the lemongrass drinks served in three-headed monkey goblets to the real jasmine bracelets, this place oozes a heartfelt welcome.

Angkor Wat, aka 'Temple City', covers more than 400 acres, surrounded by dense jungle. As the world's largest religious site, it draws crowds every day from before dawn. There's something quite magical about being there to watch the sun rise, a hushed sense of awe, even if you are sharing the spectacle with thousands. Afterwards, you can walk the passageways, clamber stone steps, witness Buddhist blessings and keep an eye out for howler monkeys in the grounds.

We were privileged to have an early morning private Buddhist lotus blessing organised by Mrs Tan Sotho, who runs the hotel. Kneeling before robed monks, I closed my eyes as they chanted, lost in the serenity of the moment. Then the flower-flinging started. A bona fide part of the ceremony, it brought me back to earth with a thump, albeit scented, to which the only response was to clasp my hands together and bow in gratitude, wondering if there wasn't a hint of mischief in these holy men! You can spend days among the temples, marvelling at the 12th-century Hindu and Buddhist architecture and bas-relief carvings. For a real sense of adventure, beat the crowds and get an early start on two wheels — it's not for the faint-hearted but it's brilliant fun — you might sprout a few more grey hairs but you'll feel decades younger. Swinging my leg over a Vespa Adventures scooter, a lovely young woman deftly whizzed me along rutted jungle paths, to the north stone gateway of Ta Prohm, the temple that is best known from the *Tomb Raider* film. Next, we sped along to Ta Nei, a small temple tucked away in the jungle. Amid the birdsong, workers were busy sweeping up leaves and setting light to them on bonfires dotted around the perimeter, sending up atmospheric wisps of smoke. Another amazing temple is Banteay Srei aka Fortress of the Women, which has such fine carving that legends say it was worked by the delicate hands of women.

Being close to these magnificent temples is humbling — they're a remarkable feat of human endeavour. As is the way the Cambodian people have moved on from their troubled past to welcome visitors with a sense of fun, openness and a generosity of spirit. In the post-coronavirus world, every holiday there will help them on the road to recovery, and it will give visitors the chance to explore this fabulous country without the crowds.

GETTING THERE

Audley Travel offers tailor-made trips to Vietnam and Cambodia with flights via Vietnam Airlines; audleytravel.com, 01993 838 100

Off the beaten TRACK

60 miles from the bustle of Ho Chi Minh City lies Ho Tram Beach – an oasis of calm on the coast of Vietnam. Tanya Pearey and family paid a visit…

We were in need of respite. I'd just dragged my family 1,500 miles the length of Vietnam, from its northern capital Hanoi down south to its frenetic financial centre Ho Chi Minh City (formerly Saigon).

Over 10 days we had taken in the limestone beauty of Halong Bay, the lush greenery of the Sa Pa mountains, the ancient history of Hue, the flickering lanterns of Hoi An and the war-ravaged Cu Chi tunnels, by way of train, plane and automobile – alongside the odd sleeper coach, minibus and our own two trusty (but often weary) legs. After all the history, culture and hours in transit, it was time for a rest…

Top-end retreat

Melia Ho Tram Beach Resort is a new five-star, 17-hectare retreat, opened this June, a two-hour drive from Ho Chi Minh City – the resort runs a free shuttle bus there and back daily. As the moped-choked city streets gradually gave way to the roadside stalls of the tiny tranquil beach town, I swear I heard the low hiss of my family starting to decompress.

After a quick dip in our pool (all the resort's villas have private pools) we were revived enough for supper at the beach-front Breeza Beach Club. It serves delicious Western food throughout the day and evening with a South-East Asian twist. Upstairs at the Muoi restaurant, it's more formal evening dining with a Vietnamese menu.

Sunrise t'ai chi

So recharged did we feel, that my teenage daughters and I were up early next morning for sunrise t'ai chi on the beach – just part of a full programme of free activities.

'I'm not sure I'm going to be any good at this,' said my eldest as we headed down. 'Don't worry,' I assured her. 'None of us will be any good but it's so early

OFF THE BEATEN TRACK

there'll be no one around to witness our rookie efforts.'

How wrong was I. The beach was buzzing with guests out for an early morning swim as us three wooden Westerners tried (and failed!) to recreate the poise and fluidity of our teacher.

'Ah yes,' the hotel manager Merry Antoja told me later. 'Asian people on the whole prefer to keep out of the sun, so they get up early for a dip to be back in the comfort of their air-conditioned villa when the sun's at its strongest.' She was right – after an 8am breakfast we barely saw a soul for the remainder of the day.

Getting active
Tennis, kayaking, paddle boarding and aqua fitness were included in the resort's free daily activities. There's a kids club too (with a separate activity programme), but the sun loungers looked too inviting. So, we ventured to the beach-front pool – the perfect place to unwind.

We visited Ho Tram in August – the beginning of the off-season in South Vietnam – and there was a strong breeze off the sea throughout our stay. It was a welcome relief after the humidity of the rest of Vietnam but made the sea a bit too rough for us to venture in.

Each day the sun rises to the left and sets to the right, in an arc over the East Sea. And it's all too easy to do nothing all day except sit and watch its progress.

Touch of luxury
There's a 10 treatment-roomed spa to tempt you away from the beach. I thoroughly enjoyed the full-body massage. And our family borrowed bicycles (free to guests) to explore the resort but it's so tranquil and tropical here that you don't really want to do anything more than sit around and appreciate it.

Melia Ho Tram offers 61 sumptuous villas (two-, three- and four bedroomed) and 152 rooms in the Tower, which are all sea-facing. Stay in a villa and, as well as your private pool, you get access to the exclusive Level pool as well as the general pool, with its swim-up bar.

It's the little details which tell you that you've truly landed in the lap of luxury – a pillow menu, an outdoor shower and a floating breakfast that you order to be delivered each morning to your villa on a buoyant tray for dining in your pool.

Fast developing
Ho Tram is positioning itself as Ho Chi Minh City's answer to New York's Hamptons – the go-to get-away for the city's well-heeled in search of top-end restoration without having to travel too far. The Melia resort certainly has the credentials – 500 metres of ocean frontage, nestling between mangrove forests and the Ray River – a canvas of blue (where sky meets sea, pool and natural lakes) splodged green with grass, coconut palms and lily pads.

The glory of the surrounding natural beauty is rounded off with top-notch service and facilities, alongside the light, airy and roomy, well-designed modern villas and rooms.

But unlike the Hamptons, there's little else around. Development is happening – on the beachfront next door to the Melia resort is wasteland cleared ready for a shopping and restaurant complex. The aim is to offer more to entice people to stay longer – the usual stay is two or three nights often tacked on to the end of a busy sight-seeing trip to this stunningly beautiful country, which is fast-expanding as a top travel destination.

But in a way, the development would be a shame. The beauty and charm of this location is that it's not built-up and bustling. Get there and experience it before it really takes off...

GETTING THERE

- For more information about Melia Ho Tram Beach Resort and to book a stay, visit melia.com, email info@meliahotram.com or call +84 (0) 254 3789 000
- For stays in Ho Chi Minh City before and after, the Fusion Suites Sai Gon is an all-suites hotel in district one, close to central sights such as the Independence Palace and War Remnants Museum, and convenient for transport. Visit fusionresorts.com, email info@fusionresorts.com or call +84 (0) 283 910 1000

Lounge in style

Tanya and family appreciated the chances to unwind

Stay in a villa right on the beach

MINDFUL TRAVEL | 109

Million pound MOUNTAINS

Dubai isn't just glitzy high-rises and boozy brunches, as Lucy Gornall discovered when she and her mum embarked on an active Emirates break…

When thinking about Dubai, you probably think skyscrapers, one-of-a-kind hotels and insane amounts of money, right? And while that's definitely the case in Dubai city itself, there is another, completely different side to this Arab emirate, one which I was keen to explore when I embarked upon a recent bonding mini break with my mother. So before taking in the more traditional bright lights of the city, we opted for some time in nearby Hatta.

Hatta is an enclave of Dubai, an hour away from the bustling city itself, high in the Hajar Mountains. It's fairly unknown, but as we discovered, spending time there is a great way to add some outdoor activity into a holiday that could otherwise have ended up almost entirely poolside.

Landing in Dubai after a seven-hour flight, it was a short cab journey to Hatta Wadi Hub, an activity centre like no other thanks to its endless choice of things to do. It's also home to the new Damani Lodges resort. Set on the rugged mountainside, there are 20 lodges, well spaced out from each other, each showing off a metal, rustic design that allows them to blend in perfectly with the surroundings.

Our lodge was stylish but simple – a large shower, comfortable beds and plain wooden interiors, as well as a balcony overlooking the activity centre down in the valley. It's cosy, and you feel like you could be in the middle of nowhere. When we weren't getting active, Mum and I enjoyed time lounging on outdoor beanbags, reading and catching up without any pressures of daily life.

Activities galore

When it came to exercise, we were spoilt for choice here. If hiking's your thing there are some great guided tours on offer, with new routes being added all the time. Be warned though, some of them are pretty challenging. My mum is fairly active and enjoys walking, but she did have to take the odd pit stop, although this isn't such a problem when a pit stop can involve looking out over miles of empty mountain-land. Without one of the experienced guides we would have been clueless as to our whereabouts – each guide knows the area like the back of their hand. A word of advice though – even at 9.30am, temperatures are soaring and the sun is strong, so high SPF, a full bottle of water and a sun hat are essential.

If you're an adrenaline junkie, this is definitely the place for you, with guided mountain biking tours, go-karts and a range of water sports on the Hatta dam ranging from kayaking – great for an upper body workout – pedal kayaks and even the classic pedalo. Most activities come at an extra cost, so we

MILLION POUND MOUNTAINS

were selective. But feeling particularly brave one morning, Mum and I agreed to take part in a Zorbing session. If this is a new one to you, just imagine rolling down a steep hill in a huge, inflatable, clear ball, partially filled with water. It might sound terrifying, but it was hilarious and Mum (surprisingly) absolutely loved it!

Not for the faint-hearted is free falling – essentially a less-intense bungee jump, but still a heart-in-mouth moment as you step off a high platform attached to a bungee, with nothing below you other than flat ground.

There is also a host of free activities on site, including plenty of family-friendly options from huge zip wires to trampolines. If you need suggestions on what will work for you and your family, the super-helpful staff at the resort go out of their way to advise you on the best things for you.

The focus here is very much on the outdoors rather than fine dining. There are some simple but tasty outlets at Wadi Hub – mostly from a selection of street-food style vans and a café. If these don't float your boat, there are healthy takeaways in the vicinity, which can be delivered to the door of your lodge. A good night's sleep is definitely required after a day of adrenaline, and the resort's peaceful location makes it the perfect place to catch up on lost hours.

Enjoying a pedalo in the

Hitting the city

Refreshed after two days in Hatta, we were ready for ultra relaxation, so headed to the city to enjoy a few days at the beautiful five-star Anantara The Palm resort.

This isn't your average resort. It's enormous and the main pool looks out over the sea, giving you the best of both worlds – a sea view without the sand-in-your-pants situation.

Our room was a large twin, the balcony of which looked out over the resort's other, quieter pool; a calm oasis. Inside, the room had a large walk-in shower room, oversized beds and plenty of "space" – Mum and I never felt like we were living on top of each other.

And if we were sick of too much mum and daughter time? The resort provides the perfect balance of relaxation vs activity. There's a 50m infinity pool, two outdoor tennis courts and even beach volleyball.

What's more, the gym was so brilliantly equipped that I actually wanted to spend a daily 30 minutes out of the sun, alone, breaking a sweat. Mum, on the other hand, preferred to relax to the max. The on-site spa is a blissful sanctuary and the Anantara Signature Massage is a must-try – 60 minutes of purpose-designed movements to stimulate circulation and promote deep relaxation, perfect to soothe aches and pains and help you switch off.

There was also a wide range of food options available, from indulgent dishes to delicious fresh healthy meals. Breakfast includes healthy "shots", roasted vegetables and every form of free-from bread imaginable. So it's safe to say all diets are catered for.

For lunch and dinner, we enjoyed salads at The Beach House eatery, and the resort's signature restaurant, Mekong, was perfect for fresh fish and meat dishes. There were plenty of cocktails too… but then life's about balance, after all!

Before heading back to the UK, we took time to experience a final thrill Dubai-style. The XLine Dubai Marina is a 1km zip wire with a difference and offers amazing views as you fly through skyscrapers and over the Dubai Marina at speeds of up to 80km/h, in a spiderman harness. It's not for the faint-hearted but on the 170m high launch platform, the view of Dubai is unreal. If anything, sign up for the XLine just to see the views, get snap-happy and round off your trip on a high (quite literally!).

Dubai from the XLine – stunning if a little terrifying for some

Getting away from it all on the edge of the city at the Anantara

Need to know
✢ To find out more about Damani Lodges and to book at Hatta Wadi Hub Visit visithatta.com
✢ For more information about Anantara The Palm Resort Dubai and to book a stay visit anantara.com/en
✢ Return flights to Dubai with Emirates can be booked on emirates.com

Living LA DOLCE VITA

We've sampled some of Italy's finest treasures, from sparkling seas and lakes, to cities bursting with history and culture

LIVING LA DOLCE VITA

Clockwise from top: Bellagio town on Lake Como (also seen on previous spread); the Mandarin Oriental Lago di Como exterior; the hotel's stylish lakefront lawn

PERFECT FOR Natural beauty

Unwind at LAKE COMO

Ultimate glamour meets fabulous scenery on the shores of Lake Como.

There's something irresistibly seductive about the power of music – and back in the 1820s, Italian opera star Giuditta Pasta (yes, Pasta) sat beneath a cypress tree in her villa's garden on the shore of Lake Como to rehearse a song.

Across the lake, the equally celebrated composer Vincenzo Bellini heard the thrilling voice echoing across the water and was enchanted. It was the start of a heady love affair that inspired his opera, *Norma*. The magical air of romance, scented with jasmine and mimosa, still lingers in the stunning surroundings of the villa, now lovingly restored to glory as a Mandarin Oriental hotel.

It has had a complete facelift over the past year, with blues and greens bringing the colours of the lake into the interiors. There's a Time Ritual spa and, best of all, an outdoor pool floating on the lake.

For anyone new to the Italian Lakes, the drive down to the shore of Como is simply breathtaking, with snow-capped mountains in the distance and clear blue skies over the rippling water.

The lake's timeless appeal still attracts celebrities to this day. Boat taxis give a wide berth to the gorgeous lakeside home owned by George and Amal Clooney – there's a hefty fine for anyone who sails too close – but they all speak very highly of their world-famous resident who has brought even more glamour to the area.

A half-hour trip across the water takes you to Bellagio, and the must-see villa, with its magnificent lake views. It's also a hotspot for weddings, though guests have to be prepared for a steep climb.

For a gastronomic treat nearer to the Mandarin Oriental, take a five-minute boat transfer to restaurant Il Vapore, where the fabulous food, combined with a rosy sunset tinting the water, makes for a magical evening.

The town of Como has its own appeal, with waterside walks and fabulous shops brimming with Italian silks. And back at the hotel, maybe try warbling your own tune as you wander through the lush botanical gardens and enjoy the verdant surroundings. Who knows who might be listening from across the lake…

✸ **FIND OUT MORE** Visit the website at mandarinoriental.com

LIVING LA DOLCE VITA

FLORENTINE *chic*
A luxurious designer hotel makes the perfect base for exploring Florence.

Florence is a city packed with treats, from the Uffizi Gallery to Giotto's Campanile, so if you're only there for a few days, how best to see the whole city? A Tuk Tuk tour ticks all the boxes, and takes you nipping around backstreets – if you're prepared for a few bumps on the cobbles.

Baking is at the heart of Italian food, and Roberto Buonamici, now in his 70s, has been making Cantucci Tuscan biscuits since he was 13. The almond biscuits, traditionally dipped in liqueur, are delicious. During a demonstration at Pasticceria Buonamici, he coaxes the ingredients into a dough on a cool marble table, to be rolled, cut and laid on trays ready for the oven. A new studio is due to open shortly if you'd like to create your own flavours of Italy.

Art, of course, is the soul of Florence – it's home to Michelangelo's David, Botticelli's Venus and Titian's Venus of Urbino, among countless other treasures. For an exploration of Renaissance art, historian Alexandra Lawrence leads a variety of private tours around the city.

The fabulously stylish Portrait Firenze Hotel, overlooking the river Arno and the Ponte Vecchio bridge, has an impeccable fashion pedigree – it belongs to the world-famous luxury goods company Ferragamo. Stay in a suite and it's like having your own city-break flat, but with the benefit of top-notch housekeeping.

The hotel's cocktail bar mingles science and fabulous flavours, while the fusion restaurant offers an amazing selection of street food, scallops, sushi and main dishes – with a knockout salmon marinated in beetroot and sake.

After a hard day's culture, who could ask for more?

✱ **FIND OUT MORE** Visit the website at lungarnocollection.com »

Clockwise from top: Dine at the hotel's Caffè dell'Oro with views of the Ponte Vecchio; the cathedral at sundown

PERFECT FOR Food and culture

Spa heaven in SARDINIA

Discover a feast for the senses on a visit to the idyllic Mediterranean island.

Surrounded by clear turquoise sea, Sardinia is a sensory paradise, famous for white sand beaches, crystal-clear waters and natural rugged beauty. The northern coast area in particular (Porto Cervo and Costa Smeralda) is famous for its summer visitors on superyachts — Beyoncé, Gwyneth Paltrow and European royalty are among the celebrities papped here.

The romantic Hotel Capo d'Orso is the perfect haven to take in the magnificent views of panoramic Palau. A boat will pick you up from its private jetty here for a three-hour sailing trip around the Archipelago La Maddalena, where the sea is so transparent that only its depth decides each shade of blue.

Famous for its healing waters, the true Sardinian Thalasso spa experience involves submerging yourself between three pools of differing temperatures — from bath temperature to cool to cold. Each small pool is full of water jets that target your upper and lower back, all designed to relax, de-stress and strengthen your body.

Hotel Capo d'Orso is one of eight Delphina hotels in northern Sardinia, each with its own beaches and boasting several boats including a magnificent 1927 sailing boat. You can arrange a private dinner on the beach, go dolphin and whale watching or have a romantic night-time cruise. And a morning trip to the winery Ledda in the Cannigione hills overlooking Costa Smeralda is a must. It's a heady experience — even before you begin sampling the delicious local wines...

✱ FIND OUT MORE Visit the website at delphinahotels.co.uk

Clockwise from top: Outdoor pools at Hotel Capo d'Orso; dine looking out at sea; the hotel sits between two fabulous beaches

PERFECT FOR Relaxing and rejuvenation

LIVING LA DOLCE VITA

Clockwise from top: Naples during sunrise; Hotel Romeo's rooftop plunge pool; Naples is the birthplace of pizza

PERFECT FOR Exploring history

Uncovering NAPLES
Discover the city with a dramatic past and vibrant present.

Naples is sometimes thought of as a staging post en route to the Amalfi Coast or the island of Capri. But it has much to offer in its own right – as anyone gripped by the novels of Elena Ferrante will know – and it's the perfect city break to immerse yourself in culture and cuisine.

The first must-see is nearby Pompeii. In 79AD, Mount Vesuvius erupted to submerge the city and its inhabitants in clouds of volcanic ash. Today, the roads are left intact, flanked by the remains of lavish villas, more modest residences, theatres, public baths and more.

Underground Naples offers very different insights into the city's past. In the historic centre, 40 metres below the ground, is a labyrinth of tunnels begun by the ancient Greeks and Romans, who channelled water for the city. Back on ground level, the streets teem with life. Vendors sell anything from bags to trinkets, handmade puppets and flowers. Linger at cake shops selling sfogliatelle, babas and delizia al limone, and visit shops selling pasta, almond-flour taralli biscuits and all flavours of ice cream.

Naples boasts over 500 churches. The church of Gesù Nuovo, with its black stone exterior, opens into a magnificent baroque interior rich in sculpture and painting. And don't miss the Duomo, the great cathedral of Naples.

Fittingly for the birthplace of the iconic Italian treat, there are pizza restaurants everywhere in Naples. Try Pizzeria Brandi, reputed inventor of the pizza margherita.

We stayed in the five-star Hotel Romeo. Designed by Japanese architect Kenzo Tange, the luxurious 79-room accommodation faces the harbour and every comfort has been thought of, right down to the Nespresso machine in the bedroom. There are two restaurants, one with a Michelin star, a heated rooftop plunge pool with views across Naples and a basement luxury spa.

So don't pass Naples by – the city is a vibrant, 21st-century box of delights.

✳ **FIND OUT MORE** Visit the website at originaltravel.co.uk

Learn to LIVE the BELLA FIGURA!

Kamin Mohammadi on how self-care the Italian way can make you happier, healthier – and even improve your love life

Ten years ago, I was stuck in a rut. It was a glamorous rut, but a rut nonetheless. I had my dream job in publishing and a fast-paced life in London. But it did not make me happy. Worse still, it actively made me unwell: I piled on pounds of inexplicable weight in spite of all the detoxes I did, my face erupted in acne, and I was permanently tired.

Then life gave me a break. Armed with a redundancy package, a one-way ticket and not knowing a word of Italian, I went to stay in a friend's flat in Florence for a few weeks. That was ten years ago. I am still here because I fell in love: first with Italian tomatoes, then the Italian lifestyle and, finally, an Italian man – a photographer named Bernardo, whom I married last year. I'm 48 now, working as a writer, and happier than I've ever been.

As well as the extraordinary beauty, the golden light and the delicious food, what struck me when I first arrived in Florence was the way the Italians lived. They stopped to say hello on the street. They chatted with the greengrocer as they shopped. They didn't drink from plastic bottles of water on the street, nor did I ever spot a takeaway coffee cup: they popped into a café and drank standing at the bar, talking to other customers. They took their time. They were, I learnt, making *la bella figura* – a concept that demands that everything be as beautiful as possible, permeating all aspects of life.

So I emulated them, measuring out my steps to force myself to abandon my habit of rushing. I learnt to enjoy street-corner chats. I stood tall and looked up. I ate without counting calories and rediscovered the excitement of fresh seasonal produce. And the joy, which characterises the Italian attitude to life, started to seep into me, as surely as the weight fell off.

With the right know-how, it's easy to bring *la bella figura* into your life – wherever you live. Here's how…

Take it slow

When I first arrived in Florence and my unhappiness was palpable, I was advised to "let the beauty heal you". I think it did. But I would never have noticed all the beauty had I not learnt first to slow down. I discovered there's practically nothing that can't be improved by taking more time – even climbing the stairs deliberately instead of running has been proven to lose you an extra pound a month. Don't eat or drink on the go – pause, go into a café and take a minute to drink a glass of water. Seek out nature, be it a city park

Kamin in her thirties
Above: **Kamin today**

LIVE THE BELLA FIGURA!

or a tree on your street. And regularly, consciously, contemplate beauty – a painting, a wide blue sky or exquisite music. Do all of this quietly and without any purpose other than your own pleasure.

Drink olive oil

When I arrived in Florence looking haggard, my skin pockmarked with acne scars, I was advised to copy Sophia Loren and take four tablespoons of oil a day. Within two weeks, the change was obvious – my skin was plump and smooth as if retouched by an expert graphic designer. My eyes sparkled, my hair was full and shiny. As if to drive the point home, I suddenly stopped being invisible to Italian men! Go for cold-pressed, single-estate extra virgin, and check how good it is by shaking the bottle – the more bubbles, the better.

Don't go to the gym

Forget the image of the old Italian lady in black with a broad girth. Italian women are some of the slimmest in Europe and yet, I have never seen one jogging along the Arno river in Florence. They simply seize any opportunity to get moving. In the city, they walk or ride their bikes. In their tall palazzos they climb the stairs instead of taking the lift.

Kamin, 48, now lives just outside Florence

At the seaside, they walk the length of the beach thigh-high in water while chatting to a girlfriend, toning their thighs and sharing laughs at the same time. They have taught me to find a form of exercise that I love and bring it into my daily routine – for me, that's long walks that lift my spirits and help me notice the tiny beauties of the day.

How to eat and not put on weight

The *bella figura* way is not a diet. It is about abundance, not deprivation. Natural, fresh and wholefoods are key – and even better if picked up in a market. The real Italian diet will surprise you. As a lover of coffee, I was gratified to learn that real coffee made from good beans has more antioxidants in it than green tea, and the simple combination of pasta with homemade tomato sauce gives the exact right combination of good fats (from olive oil) and lycopene (from tomatoes) to make it a superfood! Italians take pleasure in their food. Living in Florence, I learnt it was possible to cook, lay a table and sit down with friends to share a meal in the same hour that it had taken me to gobble a sandwich mindlessly in front of my computer.

Seek connection

Don't be fooled by the remote connection offered by social media. We humans need genuine contact with others, and loneliness has been proven to be worse for health than smoking. Go back to doing things together, even if it's just a stroll in the park. The Italian way of life – with its squares thronging with all the generations and the *passeggiata* (a leisurely evening stroll) – is perfect for this.

Love yourself

Living *la dolce vita* is about extracting the best out of life, no matter what your overriding concerns are. Once you have learnt to slow down, you'll notice those small moments that make life special. Nurture and protect yourself; everything else will follow.

Bella Figura: How to Live, Love and Eat the Italian Way by Kamin Mohammadi

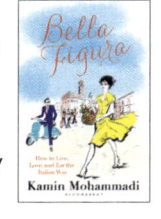

Style has nothing to do with fashion

The Italian women we idolise – Monica Bellucci (top), Gina Lollobrigida (bottom) – have style no matter what they're wearing. As Sophia Loren (middle) says: "Nothing makes a woman more beautiful than the belief that she is beautiful." I remember seeing two sprightly old ladies when I first arrived in Florence who patrolled the street every morning, arms linked, visiting each of the shops – the butcher, the greengrocer – before arriving at the café for their cappuccinos. Their cheeks were always powdered, their lipstick always on. So take out those earrings, shoes or the special dress that you love, and wear them; bring the things that make you feel beautiful into your every day – Italian women are never knowingly underdressed. Since moving to Italy, I've also experienced the transformative effect of shorter hair. Having worn it long for as long as I could remember, a few months in, and broken-hearted from a failed relationship, my hairdresser literally cut that man right out of my hair. I instantly felt lighter – and have never looked back.

RECIPE for success

For rookie chef Santa Montefiore, learning the art of Italian home cooking was the perfect antidote to her busy life

It's a hot afternoon under the Italian sun. My five friends and I sit drinking limoncello on a terrace festooned with grapes, high up in the hills with a spectacular view of the Amalfi Coast. We have just feasted on an Italian banquet of such deliciousness, cooked by the fabulous and feisty Mamma Agata, who has spent the day sharing her culinary secrets, and are sleepy and a little tipsy. It is heaven. Who would have thought that I – who will do anything to avoid cooking a meal – would be here at Mamma Agata's famed cookery school in Ravello?

When I told my book club of five girlfriends that I was going to base my next novel in Italy, Wendy – possibly the most spirited of the group – decided I needed help with the research, and that a group trip to Ravello would be just the thing to inspire me. She suggested Mamma Agata's Cookery School, having done the course herself a few years before. "You won't find anything like it anywhere," she said determinedly. "It's a magical experience you will never forget." Cooking is not one of my USPs. However, saying no to Wendy was not an option!

There was also another reason I did not decline. I'm a mother of two, and my life has been punctuated by school holidays and writing deadlines for the past 20 years. I realise now, as I get older, that I need to add variety to my life to stop it becoming *Groundhog Day* stagnant. I need to stimulate my senses. I need new places, new languages, new sounds and smells to fuel my imagination. Ravello would certainly do that.

Ravishing Ravello

The other girls needed no persuading to spend four days in the sunshine eating pasta, and so, on a drizzly grey English day at the beginning of September, we set off for Italy's resplendent Amalfi Coast. We had booked into a small pensione on the waterfront below Ravello, which is a short drive up narrow winding lanes into the hills, and it was there that we sat, on a terrace laced with honeysuckle and vines, and drank our first Prosecco. The sea glittered before us under an enormous yellow sun and Luigi, the handsome Italian proprietor, asked us questions in broken English about the nature of our trip. When we

RECIPE FOR SUCCESS

Santa learning how to cook Italian food with Mamma Agata and the rest of the class in Ravello

told him we were going to spend the day at Mamma Agata's, we did not need to elaborate. His face warmed, his eyes misted and his smile was one of knowing life's most treasured secret. We knew we were in for a treat.

Ravello is an ancient town founded in the 5th century on the crest of a magnificent hill. It boasts a 13th-century church, grand palazzi once belonging to wealthy mercantile families and stunning gardens. But I would say that Mamma Agata's is the jewel in its crown. Hers is a large house that clings to the hillside with a spectacular 180-degree view of the Amalfi Coast.

The six of us arrived the following morning and were greeted by Mamma Agata's daughter, Chiara. Chiara is sturdy with short black hair, twinkling eyes brimming with humour and affection, and a vivacious personality. She showed us to the kitchen and there stood the famous Mamma Agata. She did not say a word, she just stood, diminutive and stout like a little teapot, with a shy smile on her sweet face, exuding the charisma of a woman who has been queen of her domain for decades.

Chiara told us that her mother does not speak English. "But one has to be careful," she said, a mischievous glint in her eye. "Because there are words she does understand. For example, if I say 'mic-ro-wave'..." At that point Mamma Agata's gentle face transformed into a furious scowl and she slapped the middle of her arm with one hand and lifted the other in a tight fist, gesticulating, as only the Italians can, to silently communicate an unspeakably rude word. Of course we all laughed, the ice was broken between the students, and Mamma Agata's mouth twitched at the corners to suggest that this was a well-practised joke that always had the desired effect.

We observed and took notes while Mamma Agata cooked and Chiara explained what she was doing. It was fascinating to watch an old Italian woman who has cooked all her life throw the most delicious dishes together with mesmerising ease. The measuring of ingredients is by feel alone and there are no recipes, just instinct. I knew instantly that this mother-daughter combination would make an excellent novel, and started scribbling.

> "I needed to stimulate my senses... Ravello would do that"

Showing off my new skills

I have never been a good cook. But with Mamma Agata I learned to make a proper Bolognese sauce, a delicious Napoli sauce and a truly delectable lemon cake. But I think Mamma Agata's greatest gift is enthusiasm, and that's not something you can learn from a cookery book.

I now love cooking these dishes not only because I'm confident I can pull them off, but also because I think of Chiara and Mamma Agata whenever I do so, and they make me feel warm inside. Sometimes life throws up something extraordinary – and a moment's experience can infuse the rest of your life with a special magic.

✢ *The Temptation of Gracie* by Santa Montefiore (Simon & Schuster) is out now; to find out more about Mamma Agata's Cooking School, visit mammaagata.com

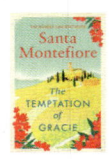

THREE COOKERY SCHOOLS CLOSER TO HOME

1 Originally founded by Prue Leith in 1975, Leiths – based in London – is widely considered one of the country's best cookery schools. Courses range from beginner to professional level, and alumni include Lorraine Pascale, Rachel Khoo and, it is rumoured, the Duchess of Cambridge. leiths.com; 020 8749 6400

2 Irish celebrity chef Darina Allen is behind Ballymaloe in County Cork, an acclaimed school set in its own glorious 100-acre organic farm and gardens with courses to suit all levels. cookingisfun.ie; +353 21 464 6785

3 On the Devon-Dorset border, River Cottage – now famous from the eponymous TV series – is an organic smallholding running courses to suit everyone (from cooking fish to hedgerow foraging) and every age. rivercottage.net; 01297 630300

Three GO MAD IN IBIZA

Fiona Gibson on reinventing the girls' holiday now the children have left home

Back in the 80s, I landed a job in an office that was 100% fun. All young, free and single, my workmates and I were up for adventures and laughs. Wham!'s *Club Tropicana* blasted out from the office stereo, and after work I'd hit the Soho pubs with my new work buddies, Kath and Jenny. "Why don't we all go on holiday together?" Jenny suggested one night. She might as well have added: and shall we keep on doing it for the next 33 years? Because that's what we've done – despite having notched up four weddings (I've had two) and seven children, and the 400 miles that separate us (while I'm based in Glasgow, my friends live in London and Kent).

In our early twenties, we'd nip off for raucous weekends to Amsterdam, Florence, Barcelona and Berlin. Who cared if a bare lightbulb dangled from our grubby hotel room, or if the scary reception lady looked disgusted when we tumbled in? We'd be out bar-hopping until dawn, dancing, flirting, surviving on coffee and gut-stripping wines, mopped up with bread whenever our energy levels started to falter.

The kiddie chaos years

By our mid-thirties, jaunting off together was no longer as simple as throwing a passport, knickers, curling tongs (yes!) and vast quantities of make-up into our bags. We were all mothers now, and so began 15 years of chaotic but wonderful holidays with our kids in various Yorkshire cottages (husbands were left at home). While our children played freely on beaches, we three friends caught up with each other's lives. Shattered but happy, we'd all tumble back to the cottage.

I loved these holidays. As younger women we'd helped each other through heady love affairs and dramatic break-ups, and now we relished an "all in this together" sense around motherhood too. I wanted these trips to continue forever – but, one year, my twin sons announced that they did not. Couldn't they be bribed with handfuls of coppers for Scarborough's penny arcades, or the promise of donkey rides on the beach? "No, Mum," one of my boys sighed, when I'd resorted to begging, "because I am 17 years old."

Gradually, all the other children bailed out too. In our early fifties now, Jenny, Kath and I were seemingly redundant while our offspring embarked on adventures of their own. "We could still go away," Jenny suggested.

"But the kids think we're embarrassing and tedious," I pointed out. "They don't even want to do the Whitby Dracula tour."

"No," she said, 'I don't mean a donkeys-and-Dracula kind of holiday. I mean the three of us. Just... us."

Now that sounded enticing... and also rather naughty, to go away unencumbered by children just for – you know – fun. "Maybe we could meet at a Travelodge somewhere halfway?" I

> "In our twenties we'd be bar-hopping until dawn, dancing and flirting"

Jenny, Kath and Fiona on holiday

THREE GO MAD IN IBIZA

suggested, tentatively. Stuff that, my friends retorted. We were off to Ibiza, I was to shop for non-industrial swimwear and leave my hair shirt at home. And so we headed, not to a chain hotel off the M6, but Santa Eulalia, on Ibiza's east coast.

Now it's all about us

As we arrived at the spa hotel of Aguas de Ibiza, I remembered the whole point of going away with one's best women friends. It's to relish maximum uninterrupted time together – hence our requested three-bed room – and to simply kick back, with no demands whatsoever. While families are welcome at the hotel, its relaxed luxury vibe is perfect for couples or a bunch of friends like us who, actually, deserve a treat.

Poolside, we lazed and we chatted, pausing only to be handed some delicious treat by a passing waiter (a plate of tiny pastries with drinks, or dinky skewers of pineapple). In those Yorkshire cottages we'd cook up vats of spag bol, or roast three chickens, and dole it all out like in a school canteen. Here at our hotel's outdoor restaurant, as we lingered over squid, lobster, salads garnished with flowers and exquisite desserts, we decided that we really didn't miss everyone back home terribly much at all.

I had a heavenly massage in the dreamy spa, and we all felt obliged to take in the eye-popping view (and several cocktails) from the hotel's rooftop bar where, conveniently, there is another pool, for adults only. And while we might not have been chasing flirty-eyed waiters this time, we happened to note that the staff, who wafted around in white linen pyjama-style uniforms, were as eye-pleasing as the island itself.

When we could bear to venture beyond the hotel, we explored Ibiza Town itself, its twisting streets wending between the beautifully sun-faded houses and alluring tapas bars.

Dancing the night away

We loved laid-back Santa Eulalia, the perfect town if you're more into relaxing than whooping it up every night, and shopped for pom-pom-embellished baskets and delicate jewellery. The Ibiza vibe here is the right side of hippy – less batik trousers, more floaty linen and cottons instead, and so achingly pretty that you just want to buy everything, whether or not it would be befitting Glasgow's grey skies.

Cala Nova beach, with its silky sand and scattering of restaurants, was well worth the 15-minute taxi hop. All of this was a world away from San Antonio, the island's clubbing capital, the thought of which had triggered a nervous rash when my friends had first mooted Ibiza as a destination. In fact there's far more to "the white isle" than partying all night, although we do find ourselves venturing to Pikes Hotel (pikesibiza.com), the infamous venue for Freddie Mercury's 41st birthday bash, from which the firework display could be seen in Majorca. It was also the location for Wham!'s *Club Tropicana* video.

Here, fuelled by espresso martinis, we somehow found ourselves dancing for hours, until I stopped and noticed that it was actually... daylight. I hadn't danced all night since I was 20. How could this be possible? Then I looked at the two friends beside me, who have been my partners in crime for our entire adult lives, and thought: oh. So, what are we doing next year?

✢ *Aguas de Ibiza is a member of Small Luxury Hotels of the World. To book, visit slh.com*
✢ *Fiona's new novel,* The Mum Who'd Had Enough *(Avon), is out now*

> "Going away with your best friends is about relishing maximum time together"

Making time to share a drink...

...kick back and relax

MOUNTAIN MAYHEM!

Would an Austrian activity holiday answer the quest for a suits-all-ages break? Miranda McMinn found out

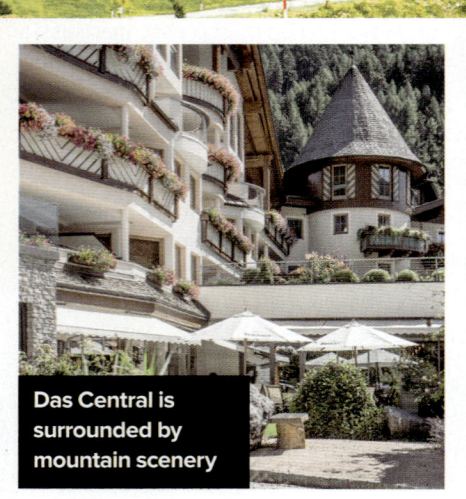

Das Central is surrounded by mountain scenery

One year, we thought it was time to try out a different kind of holiday. Like many a British family, come summer, we generally flock like homing pigeons to an eye-wateringly expensive villa somewhere in the Med. Obviously, this is something we adore doing, but we are ready for a change from meeting the challenges of supermarket shopping in 40-degree heat and coming up with ways to entertain the youth — our girls aged eight, 11 and 18. Because there's nothing like lying back on a sunlounger and finally breathing out after approximately 50 weeks of stress, then hearing the strains of 'Stop it!' or 'Get out of my room!' and 'Leave me alone, I hate you,' wafting across the balmy breeze. You know you've then got approximately 10 seconds before someone turns up at your feet saying 'I'm bored' and you blow a gasket. Or is that just me?

We're ready to try anything to keep everyone out of mischief, but we truly

Left: Lush Alpine mountain views on a sunny day; *Below:* Aqua Dome Spa; Miranda enjoys chilling out

don't know what to expect from Austria. We're not a particularly sporty family, but we are active — when at home we all walk and swim. And who doesn't love staying in a hotel — crisp sheets, beds made, and unfeasibly calorific breakfasts that you don't have to cook or wash up after?

An hour's drive down the Ötztal Valley through Alpine villages complete with flower-filled balconies (which, in some areas, we discover later, are compulsory), and we are in Sölden, pulling up outside Das Central. Hotel costs in summer are much lower than they are in winter ski season, so once-unattainable luxury is more of a possibility — plus we are given Ötztal Premium Cards, giving us free access to cable cars, public bus services, waterparks and other activities throughout the valley.

Das Central is five stars and does not disappoint. Marble floors, check. Huge rooms with requisite comfortable beds and — in our room — a bath big enough for two, check. Attractive staff wearing traditional dirndls, check. Next, onto the activities. Yes, had I mentioned that we are on that most unglamorous-sounding thing, an activity holiday? But before you say 'ugh' and roll your eyes, let me explain. The goal here is relaxation and, by our age we all know (as the Austrians have done for centuries), that the number one way to relax is by taking exercise in a natural setting, breathing in air worthy of paradise, getting slightly fatigued and then coming back and hitting the spa.

And what a spa! There's a pool plus 10 saunas and steam rooms across a variety of themes. There are multiple places to relax — recliners of every sort in every setting, including outside on a tiny lawn with a 360-degree view of the mountains that is frankly taking the biscuit (did someone say biscuits? Yes, there are plenty of snacks in the spa too!). We end our day of travel watching the sun set behind the mountains from a cushioned recliner. So far, things could be worse.

On day one we start with a child-friendly hike (one of the hotel's daily timetable of free activities including guided hikes and exercise classes), led by the lovely Wolfgang, who brings along his young daughter. Wolfgang has the biggest calves I have ever seen. He leads us mountain novices gently up into the forest, taking regular stops to catch our breath. We cross the thundering icy river, walk beside waterfalls and rocks covered with the >>

> "Our mountain walking guide, Wolfgang, has the biggest calves"

MOUNTAIN MAYHEM!

MINDFUL TRAVEL | 125

kind of Alpine plants I've only ever seen before at the garden centre.

By the time we get back we have notched up 7km and – get this – 42 floors on my phone's fitness app. We are back just in time for what Das Central calls 'a snack' (included in the price and available daily from 2.30-5pm), but what we would commonly call lunch. Face-stuffing is a major factor here – that's what all the 'activity' is in aid of. Later we indulge in a five-course dinner in the smart main hotel restaurant, where the wine list is like a telephone directory, with something to suit every pocket.

The next day is cloudy and rather cold, but instead of worrying about this we make like the locals and simply head for the nearby Aqua Dome, a thermal spa fed by warm bubbling water that springs directly from the mountains at 104F (40C). It is a real cultural experience – crowded but spotlessly clean. Afterwards my skin glows.

I'm not going to lie, I'm dreading the next day's activity – 'e-biking'. However I gear myself up and, surprise surprise, it is fantastic! Most 'bikers' come to the area to go berserk on the trails up in the mountains, but there is a cycle-only lane from Sölden to Längenfeld and, after a slow start biking around the car park with our guide, Lily, we get in the swing. e-biking is brilliant, it turns out, because while you pedal you can, if you want, just give yourself a bit of an extra 'wheeeee' factor by using some battery, so going uphill is as much fun as cycling on the flat. Parts of the trail take us into the mountains, pine forests and flower-filled, thyme-scented meadows, past churches with ornate painted walls and unusual features, such as wooden tiles.

A must on a visit to this area is 007 Elements, a James Bond museum 9,850ft (3,000m) above sea level, where stunt-filled chunks of *Spectre* were filmed. Up here you feel much colder, and pick your way from the top of the bubble lift through a rocky, lunar landscape to a concrete, Bond-themed lair. Here, you experience the full 007 trip through a series of 'installations' – films of the cast and crew, including a sequence in a hall of mirrors. There are technical reconstructions of stunts, plus artefacts and costumes, including the golden gun itself. The restaurant, ice Q, is a cantilevered glass box that hangs out

> "e-biking is brilliant because you can give yourself a bit of an extra "wheeee" factor"

over a heady drop, and is the most dramatic place I have ever eaten lunch – we try Austrian classics including Wiener schnitzel and Sachertorte. Afterwards we walk it off with an 'easy' hike. We follow a footpath through the piney mountainside, chasing butterflies and jumping across brooks, while the odd mountain biker hurtles past on the alarmingly narrow track. Back at the hotel, we hit the spa and let the steam and saunas soothe our limbs. Even the kids realise how great all this is making us feel. We've got a family of walkers on our hands!

The last of our adventures is Area 47, about 35 minutes drive away and billed as 'a playground for adults'. We have been signed up for rafting and I have some serious misgivings, not improved when I sign the lengthy waiver form, but – guess what? – it's utterly brilliant. The female instructor briefs us on a few instructions and we hit the water. Almost immediately we are flying through rapids with ice-cold waves of water crashing over our heads, but instead of grimacing as I'd imagined, we're all laughing our heads off. Then the girls go mad on the craziest waterslides I've ever seen, including a vertical drop and a cannon that shoots you into the water. I get seriously sunburnt – the temperature today is 24 degrees – and we leave feeling elated.

That night we dine in the hotel's ultra-smart Ötztaler Stube. My husband and the girls are under strict instructions to 'behave'. Thankfully, we make the grade. The wood-panelled room is lined with pictures of Alpine scenes past and food is brought on trays made of stags' antlers. The meal is around 10 courses, when you include all the amuse-bouches and petits fours. It's going to be a serious comedown going home. But the return journey finds us all feeling rebuilt – healthy, relaxed, smooth-skinned and, after all that exercise, my belt is, incredibly, on the same notch as it was when I arrived, in spite of all my greed. Now that is what I call a result!

✢ **Find out more** Das Central, Sölden, Austria, has double rooms available on a half-board basis. All guests receive the Ötztal Premium Card. Visit central-soelden.com for further information

Edgy: Check out the 007 Elements James Bond museum

Fight the rapids on an Area 47 rafting adventure

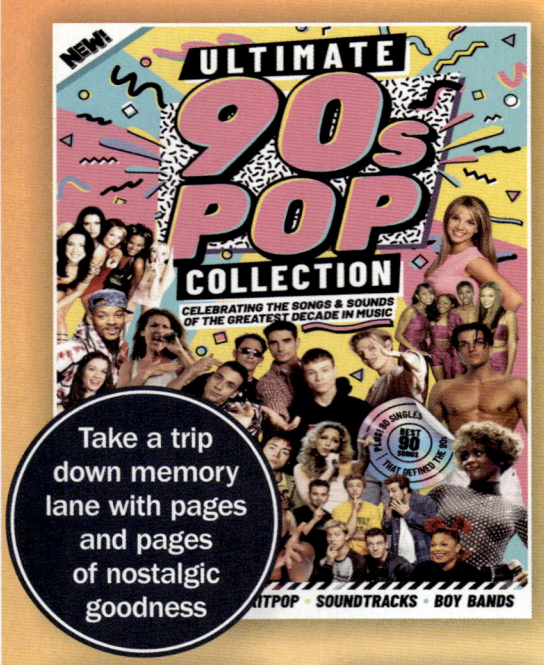

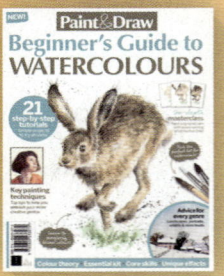

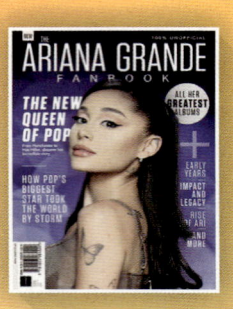

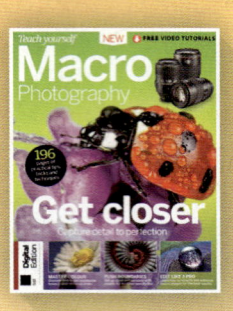

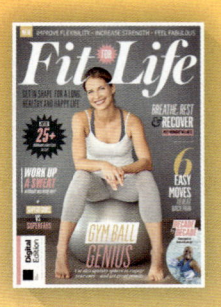

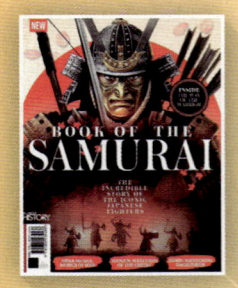

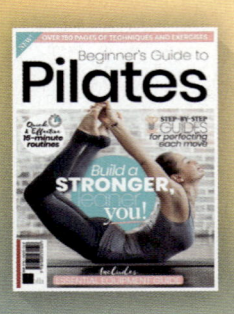

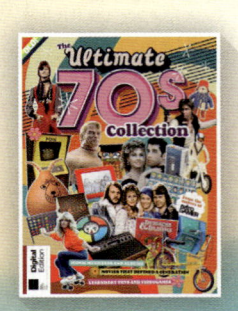

Take a trip down memory lane with pages and pages of nostalgic goodness

Get up close and personal with your favourite bands and artists

Find inspiration and impress your dinner guests with recipes for every occasion

✓ Get great savings when you buy direct from us

✓ 1000s of great titles, many not available anywhere else

✓ World-wide delivery and super-safe ordering

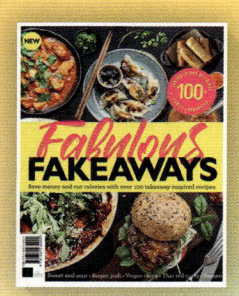

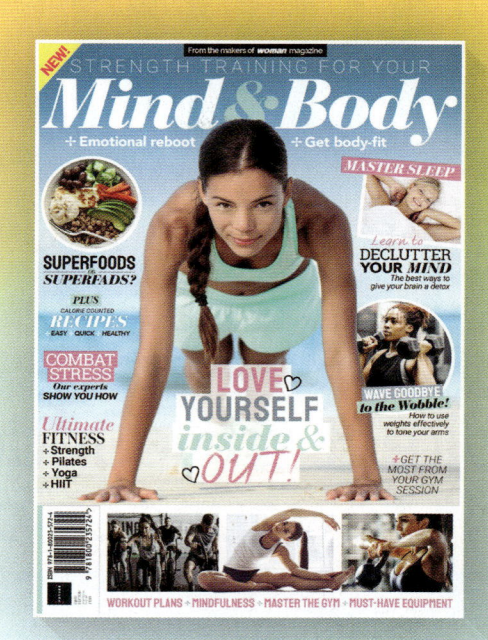

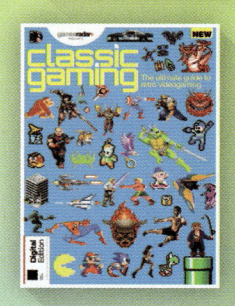

DISCOVER OUR GREAT BOOKAZINES

From history and music to gaming and cooking, pick up a book that will take your hobby to the next level

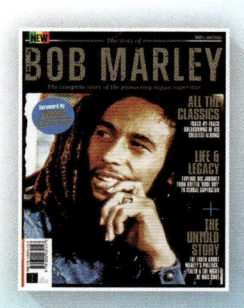

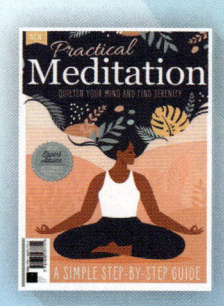

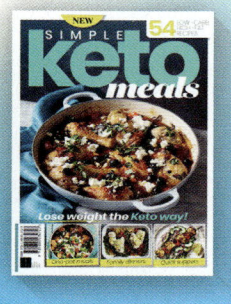

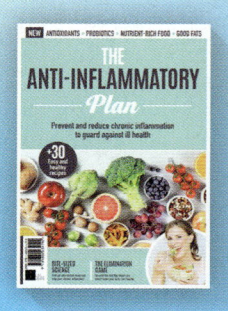

Discover fun facts and get creative with kids' activity books

Follow us on Instagram 📷 @futurebookazines

FUTURE www.magazinesdirect.com
Magazines, back issues & bookazines.

SUBSCRIBE & SAVE UP TO 61%

Delivered direct to your door or straight to your device

Choose from over 80 magazines and make great savings off the store price!

Binders, books and back issues also available

Simply visit www.magazinesdirect.com

- ✓ No hidden costs
- 🚚 Shipping included in all prices
- 🌐 We deliver to over 100 countries
- 🔒 Secure online payment

FUTURE **magazinesdirect.com**
Official Magazine Subscription Store